MW00913959

This Pilgrim Priest

Recollections from the priesthood of Monsignor Ben Kasteel

In collaboration with Ann Krier

thispilgrim@yahoo.com
ISBN # 9780984120314
Printed by Action Printing • Lubbock, Texas

Cover design by:
Abbigail Hines, 8th Grade

media: acrylic

"I wanted to show Msgr. Ben traveling from his past to his present. I used the windmills to show the time progressing. The man symbolizing Msgr. Ben has a cross-shaped shadow. I wanted to show our faith by using the cross. After seeing pictures of the tulip, which is Holland's flower, I decided to add some tulips to represent Holland."

To: Phil Gage

Thanks for the years we spend together in Wheeling. I hear rumors that the parish will go back to the Diocese. They always want it. Thanks for all the Marish friendships over the years.

[signature]

I will appoint over you shepherds
after my own heart, who will
shepherd you wisely and
prudently.

5-23-11

Jeremiah 3:15

3

Foreword

This Pilgrim Priest is a beautiful and fitting title for this noble soul, Msgr. Ben Kasteel, Vicar General and Rector of the Cathedral of Christ the King, Lubbock. The word *pilgrim* has taken a deep meaning with Vatican Council II as the essence of the Church on her earthly journey, the Bride of Christ, full of dynamism on her journey and with hope to surely meet her Bridegroom, the Lord of History and the Lord of Love. Monsignor Ben was renewed with the same pace as the Church was being renewed by the Council. As a newly ordained priest, he travels to foreign fields for **evangelization**, whether in Samoa; Cleveland; Wheeling, West Virginia; and finally the Plains frontier of West Texas. He is genuine to his calling --- a *pilgrim* in the best sense of the word of Vatican Council II.

And the word priest has also been deepened by his own personal witness as a Pilgrim Priest, as well by the Church's magisterial writings on the priesthood. Vatican Council II focused on the identity of the fullness of the priesthood, i.e., the Bishop. Yet, it did not neglect the role of the priest as in *"Pastores Dabo Vobis"* of John Paul II. In combining the personal witness of this gentle soul and the ecclesial understanding of the priesthood in action, this Pilgrim Priest, Monsignor Ben Kasteel, Vicar General, honors the Church Universal, and in particular, this local Church --- the Diocese of Lubbock. This Pilgrim Priest makes the Catholic Church credible, approachable, and loveable for others; the Church is seen fully prophetic.

Yes, Mother Church has raised up sons skilled in priestly tasks for **evangelization** for all four corners of the world and for all times. "I will be with you until the end of time." (Matthew 28:20)

Most Rev. Placido Rodriguez, CMF
Bishop of Lubbock

Conceptual designs submitted by Christ the King Cathedral Middle School art department illustrate their interpretations of the pilgrimage.

Each chapter of Msgr. Ben's journey has three parts: an introduction summarizing the facts, time, and place;

dialogue between Msgr. Ben (B) and Ann (A) recollecting wisdom from the priesthood;

a parable or scriptural passage with commentary relating to the events and topics of that chapter.

All scripture references taken from Saint Joseph Edition of The New American Bible, Catholic Book Publishing Co., New York, 1992.

Scripture reflections at the close of each chapter represent Ann's personal thoughts and connections between Jesus' story and Msgr. Ben's pilgrimage. This commentary should not be construed as representing the Diocese of Lubbock.

Overview of the Pilgrimage

1937   Born to a farming family in the Netherlands (Holland)

1950   Entered minor seminary of the Marist Fathers in Hulst, Holland

1958   First Profession within the Society of Mary, or Marists

1964   Ordination into the priesthood among a class of seven, followed by a year of teaching at minor seminary

1965   Left Holland to serve seven mission churches in the Samoan Islands

1971   Arrived in U.S.A. as part of Marist international exchange program as associate pastor at St. Pius X Parish - Cleveland, Ohio

1973   Invited by Bishop Pio back to Samoan Islands to build team ministry

1975   Return to St. Pius X Parish in Cleveland, Ohio as associate pastor with Fr. Gene Driscoll as pastor

1979   Pastor at St. Vincent de Paul Parish - Wheeling, West Virginia

1988   Sabbatical year in Rome, Italy (Marists renewal program) and Santa Barbara, California (international School of Spirituality)

1989   Pastor at Our Lady of Guadalupe Parish - Plainview, Texas

1997   Incardinated into the Diocese of Lubbock

1998   Rector of Christ the King Cathedral - Lubbock, Texas

2004   Pope John Paul II confers the title Prelate of Honor Reverend Monsignor Bernard Kasteel

2011   Retirement after forty-seven years in the priesthood

Ordination into the priesthood — February 22, 1964
Fr. Bernard Kasteel, S.M., with his mother and father

Leading parish evangelization program at St. Pius X
Cleveland, Ohio

Celebrating 25th anniversary in the priesthood
Wheeling, West Virginia

Msgr. Gene Driscoll and Bishop Placido Rodriguez
with Msgr. Ben
Diocese of Lubbock, Texas

Reverend Monsignor Bernard Kasteel
Christ the King Cathedral
Lubbock, Texas
2004

Map of the Journey

Catherine Limboy, 7th Grade

media: watercolor; chalk pastels

"I wanted to convey how life progressed through time for Msgr. Ben through this picture."

15

CHAPTER ONE
Covenant Cornerstone

His journey began on March 8, 1937, from a small
rural homestead similar to the international settings he
would be assigned throughout his life in the priesthood.
Farm responsibilities began early and stayed late for
him and his eleven siblings, with rarely an objection
raised. In his homeland of the Netherlands, just prior
to the official onset of World War II, Bernard Kasteel
absorbed lasting impressions in this traditional Catholic
family context. Marriage was modeled for him by
parents that took seriously their sacramental vows,
as well as their understanding of home as "the first
church." Theirs was a sacred partnership committed to
the formation of their children, maintenance of the land,
and stability under the roof. Domestic assignments
came under the scrutiny of the firm and efficient
matriarch, conveying the gift of management skills her
son exemplifies today. But young Bernard (Bennie)
preferred the tasks outdoors, concerned with soil and
livestock, alongside his congenial father. Here seeds
were planted, in the land and in his heart, that fostered
a faithful perspective of harvest: one must sow in a
timely fashion; an attentive hand is required during the
cycle of growth; and soil tilled with love, patience, and
optimism increases the yield.

The Kasteel family would anticipate that one or more of the children would choose a path of religious life, as was customary in this time and place. Only his father was surprised when his dedicated farmhand, Bennie, responded to a vocational call by a missionary priest during a presentation in his Catholic elementary school. Upon hearing testimony from the priest of the need for laborers in the field, Bennie's love of land converged with his love for Christ. His father had accurately assessed his son's aptitudes for "sowing and reaping," and openly supported Bennie's decision, but silently relinquished the dream for this son to follow in his footsteps.

From these early years of nurture undergirded by the graces of a sacramental marriage, the now ordained priest, Father Ben, carried firsthand knowledge of covenant love into his ministry. He himself had been the recipient of his parents' sacrificial investments toward the welfare of each other and their twelve children. And he perceived in their commitment a pervasive understanding that God's will on earth necessitates our participation. Throughout his subsequent years in the priesthood, Fr. Ben became deeply convinced that a couple's investment in sacramental marriage facilitates a participation with God in His will for joy in our lives. Yet this conviction has been challenged over and over again in witnessing marriages not only "less than" God's best, but with unarguably disintegrated results. To this day, after forty-seven years of hearing confessions of betrayed trust and dishonesty, he remains a staunch advocate of marriage preparations as required by the Catholic diocese as the best means to overturn the odds of divorce.

Childhood farm house in the Netherlands

The Kasteel family farming operations
2004

Ann (A): During your pastorate at Christ the King Cathedral, you have seen numerous failings of couples and of the Church, in being able to halt the trend toward divorce in today's world. Why do you take so much personal interest in the preparation for and the institution of marriage?

Msgr. Ben (B): Well, as a priest, I think you experience the pain of the people, especially when hearing confessions. I hear all these people that really should be happily married, and they are unhappily married. I also hear the stories of those who have been married before and are trying to get a nullification from the church. You know they all somehow enter with the best intention into marriage. Most are sincere, but some play a trick on things. Say by example, I am surprised about the number of people that are so close to the marriage celebration, even in the Catholic Church, who are still unfaithful before marriage, who still have another relationship. One person was a clear homosexual and having another boyfriend, but his female fiance knew nothing about it. It is usually discovered after the marriage that there was no honesty at all, there was no truthfulness.

Today there is much talk about a lack of commitment, and I agree that this is also one of the reasons for so much divorce. There is very little real, lasting commitment. People easily bend out of their marriage. They feel they should be happy from the beginning, they don't think, "we have to work on it, and slowly it will become a happier relationship." So many couples are frustrated because their lifestyle of working at different times, one works all the time at night, the other works the day. . . and there are so many relationships at work that people have outside of their marriage and so on. So I think we need much more sincerity in our marriages.

A: How is the Church affected by the breakdown of traditional marriages?

B: I think it is not just the Church that is concerned, I think the state is concerned. The State of Texas may have more a financial reason of concern, but I think that government is starting to recognize the moral reasons as well. You see the hurt, the family is falling apart, all these lawsuits, so much pain involved in the process of divorce. And because the Church makes it difficult to get out of marriage, more couples start to live on a kind of civil contract together, and less people will get married in the Church.

The biggest thing for me, that I know well out of confession, is how deeply the children get hurt, the life of the children when they have to make decisions. In custody cases where siblings must decide which parent to live with, it breaks up not just their relationship with the parents, but with each other. So you see that marriage preparations try to bring a serious understanding to the couple before they face these possible tragedies. One program that the Diocese of Lubbock is bringing to assist is RETROUVAILLE (pronounced *retro-vi,* an international, laity-led intervention program for at-risk marriages), and I think that is a good start. But couples have to be willing to participate, and you rarely get one hundred percent attendance.

A: Are there cultural factors outside of the Church that would strengthen marriage preparation?

B: I think the biggest setback in marriage today is the lack of parental involvement. When the Bible speaks about the parents, get a good wife for your children, I think today the parents don't play much in it at all. Many kids get engaged at the college level, away from home. Sometimes a couple becomes engaged before meeting the other's parents. The main opinion seems to be that the marriage is between you and me. . . it also has to do with your family and my family. It has to be a family of people, family bond. I have seen marriage ceremonies where a parent doesn't even want to be there. A lot of young people don't think that a problem with the family is a major issue. They think is something small, that after marriage things will work out. Usually that is not the case.

A: Your fervor is evident when talking about this topic. Do you wish you had more time for this pastoral focus apart from administrative duties?

B: I have plenty of time. That is not the problem. The problem is that people today have made up their minds they are getting married. Most are not willing to listen very much. Some couples are the exception, and go to even more preparation than is required. But the largest number know what is required by the Church and just sit the time out. They are much more concerned about the wedding day preparations. Things have become much more materialistic. I hope the time will come when there is less of the commercial influence, and the wedding becomes much more simple. A simple wedding, then celebrate in the biggest way when you are twenty-five years married. Have a big celebration.

A: How would you describe your personal experience of learning and growing in the understanding of covenant love?

B: What I will call the cycle of marriage is an invitation of God. As God is family, we are called to create family. Like the love the Church proclaims is the love that Christ has for you, is the way you should start to love your partner. Try to think, "How is this partner loved by God?"

This morning I had Mass and scripture was from St. Paul's letter about stability and whether or not to be married, what should you do? That immediately puts another question into your mind, "For what reason should you be married?" "What is the real reason you should marry?" "Can you really love?" Because if we are so selfish, so self-centered, then marriage is all about me and it's not about you. Same thing when talking about religion, that religion is all about me, when it is all about Christ. It's not really about what is in store for my life, it's about how can I serve Christ. Covenant love is so important because God in His great love, nothing that He did in creation was for Himself. He did all of creation for us. I mean, God is perfectly happy in Himself. . . He doesn't need our joy for Himself. God likes to bring joy to us for our happiness.

A: You are pointing toward several misconceptions about both God and about marriage. Please elaborate.

B: I think in marriage we have to work on a covenant love that, even though today sounds negative, is laying down one's life for the other person. That is what I want to do, because I care so much about the other person. That's what you like to hear when a couple comes for marriage preparation, how they really care for the other person. When you feel they are really caring, that there is a dedication to the other, then there is commitment.

24

But when questions are asked during preparations about the real intentions of getting married, you already wonder . . . "Because he makes me happy," "He satisfies me." That is not covenant love. Covenant is about how God lets His sun shine upon us, in good times and in bad. How God is faithful no matter what, and how we try to imitate Christ's love in laying down His life for another . . . maybe trying to love like that in marriage. So I think there is a lot of secular thinking in marriage, and you wonder if young people understand the holy dimension when getting married in the Church.

Another aspect of covenant love that is so very important is that it is expressive. Sometimes this is overlooked because of different cultural orientations. Say in the Hispanic community there is much expression in their love for each other, whereas the Irish are more reserved. That does not mean that Irish are not as intimate, but rather have a different way of expressing. A lot of men who might say, "I love you" and mean it, fail in showing the expression of their love for the other. There must be a principal of expressing the covenant love often, and in many forms.

Covenant love is also expressed in taking care of the children. Both parents should work together to express love for their children. Making it really visible, trying to give the same signs, is part of compatibility. It is a very important issue. I'm not sure what it is, maybe college life, that leads young people to not feel a part of their family background. So many young people today come from divorced families. They have gone through the hurt of their own family getting divorces, and really want to go wholeheartedly into a new marriage. But you wonder if they are really healed of their family wounds. Say by example, so many families suffer from a history of alcohol abuse, patterned through many generations. This should be fully acknowledged and directly addressed before the couple exchanges their vows.

THE PARABLE OF THE TALENTS.
It will be as when a man who was going
on a journey called in his servants and
entrusted his possessions to them. To
one he gave five talents; to another, two;
to a third, one---to each according to his
ability. Then he went away. Immediately
the one who received five talents went and
traded with them, and made another five.
Likewise, the one who received two made
another two. But the man who received
one went off and dug a hole in the ground
and buried his master's money.

   After a long time the master of those
servants came back and settled accounts
with them. The one who had received
five talents came forward bringing the
additional five. He said, "Master, you
gave me five talents. See, I have made
five more." His master said to him, "Well
done, my good and faithful servant. Since
you were faithful in small matters, I will
give you great responsibilities. Come,
share your master's joy."

   Then the one who had received two
talents also came forward and said,
"Master, you gave me two talents. See,
I have made two more." His master
said to him, "Well done, my good and
faithful servant. Since you were faithful

in small matters, I will give you great responsibilities. Come, share your master's joy."

Then the one who had received the one talent came forward and said, "Master, I knew you were a demanding person, harvesting where you did not plant and gathering where you did not scatter; so out of fear I went off and buried your talent in the ground. Here it is back." His master said to him in reply, "You wicked, lazy servant! So you knew that I harvest where I did not plant and gather where I did not scatter? Should you not then have put my money in the bank so that I could have got it back with interest on my return? Now then! Take the talent from him and give it to the one with ten. For to everyone who has, more will be given and he will grow rich; but from the one who has not, even what he has will be taken away. And throw this useless servant into the darkness outside, where there will be wailing and grinding of teeth."

Matthew 25:14-30

The parable of talents seems to be a lesson in investment, suggesting that those who invest wisely reap the benefits of their efforts. Certainly this wisdom can be applied to marriage: those who proactively nurture the sacred vows that have been "taken," reap for themselves "profit" of lifelong dividends. Marriage, in the context of this parable, is not a static commodity to be frozen in its initial stages, as was the response of the servant who buried his talent. This implies no opportunity for growth, no vision of improvement, no desire to build upon a small beginning. Rather, it speaks of fear of failure, trying to read the other's mind, and a lazy, half-hearted approach to being given something of great potential value. Is this, indeed, a "wicked" approach to something so sacred, so valuable as the sacrament of marriage?

Better by far is the response that something given of value deserves the investment of time, attention, forethought and initiative. Too often young (and not-so-young) people have such low expectations of marriage they see only "one talent's worth" of potential in its future. From the beginning an attitude prevails of, "Oh well, if it doesn't work out, at least I will know I tried to make it work." "Tried" in this case often implies cohabitation, and rarely does it imply conversion from self-centered to agape-centered love.

Notice that in the parable, the first servant who received five talents (began with high expectations, knew the potential) went and traded with them. Imagine expecting the full potential that marriage provides, a lifetime context in which *eros*, romantic love, matures into (is traded for) *agape*, other-centered love. This is the work of the people of God, through home as the first church, as well as through sacramental marriage preparations, to lead those considering sacred vows into this spiritual understanding of matrimony. Be clear about the disregard for Christian marriage raised in contemporary culture. Raise the bar of expectation and be categorically honest about the investment --- the more Christ-like initiative that is deposited, the more the potential growth toward transformed lives and love.

Don't overlook the outcomes in the parable: the wise investors were invited to "share your master's joy;" the lazy investor was "thrown into the darkness." One does not need to look far to see these consequences a reality when applied to the principles of marriage. There is no greater joy than two lives spent in companionship, evolving in their covenant love with Creator God, witnessing their shared journey into twilight years. By contrast many have said, in the midst of a failing marriage, they are plunged into the darkness of "wailing and grinding of teeth." A pastor's heart is wrenched every time this potential for the Master's joy disintegrates, because a pastor believes so deeply in the Master's invitation to share His joy.

Nikki Diaz, 6th Grade

media: watercolor; India ink

"The windmill is shaped like a cross because I wanted to show a different windmill that's not from America, to show he's been in Holland and other countries."

33

CHAPTER TWO

Seminary Formation

In 1950, at the impressionable age of thirteen,
Bernard Kasteel left home to enroll in the minor
seminary* of the Marist Fathers in Hulst, Holland.
Within this all-male context of approximately one
hundred students, Bennie began to experience the pros
and cons of life in community. His agreeable nature
brought affirmation from teachers and students alike,
which cultivated his boyhood decision to become a
missionary priest. Many classmates returned home
to secular life, but Bennie flourished in religious
community. . . even if challenged by the untimely death
of his older brother and his struggles as a teenager to
speak, read, and translate six foreign languages.

This was a boarding school environment which
provided students away from home many normal
and expected engagements. Chores, for example,
punctuated each day, as well as an expectation to
"get along" with classmates, showing respect and
attentiveness as if each were a family member.
Team sports and physical exercise advocated
disciplined fitness as part of daily routine. And even
a consciousness of social structure thrived, in that
seminary students engaged one another in groups that
modeled civic government. Collaboration was required

in assigned tasks to improve the environment, attitude and spirit of the collective community. Leadership qualities burgeoned through electoral positions within each cluster.

Bennie had chosen the path of religious community formation, in this case the Society of Mary, or Marist, over diocesan formation for several reasons. The Marist community concentrated upon mission fields, a desire which had surfaced very early in young Bennie's life. Even though diocesan formation would have provided much of the same educational and theological training, religious formation provided an added dimension of spirituality based upon community vows and the founders' vision. As he described, the Marist spirituality centered upon the Holy Family's thirty "hidden" years in Nazareth, in which Mary, Joseph and Jesus maintained their humble, hidden and unknown daily routine. . . done in the perspective that God was at work in even the most mundane tasks. No need for fanfare, attention or accolades. Small things done with great love. To this day, the Marist spirituality suits Bernard Kasteel, witnessed in his reserved, thoroughly attentive guidance of those under his parish roof.

Minor seminary progressed through the novitiate to major seminary,* though not all of Bennie's initial group made the transition. Along the way, teachers helped these adolescent young men discern the call of God upon their lives. No doubt was left as to the choices of poverty, obedience, and celibacy in following this path. . . not to mention leaving home for a predicted fourteen years (without return home vacations), to foreign, possibly third world countries.

During these impressionable years, most teenage boys are intrigued with fostering skills for an income-producing livelihood, and with developing sexuality toward roles as husbands and fathers. Bennie spent these years counting the costs of community vows, yet remained committed, even fulfilled, in his advancing pilgrimage toward priesthood. His parents supported, yet never demanded, their son's devout path. "We hope you like the seminary, we hope you become priest. . . but our door is always open. If you would like to come back home, you are welcomed."

*Minor seminary - a secondary boarding school created for the specific purpose of enrolling teenage boys who have expressed interest in becoming priests. They are generally Roman Catholic institutions, and designed to prepare boys both academically and spiritually for vocations to the priesthood and religious life. (Wikipedia)

*Major seminary - a Roman Catholic theological college devoted to training men for the priesthood and usually offering a six-year program emphasizing philosophy and theology.
(Dictionary.com)

**Bernard
"Bennie" Kasteel**
Minor Seminary of
the Marist Fathers
Hulst, Holland 1950

Classmates making first profession at minor seminary
September 12, 1958
Ben Kasteel - kneeling, fifth from left
Note: Bishop from Solomon Islands - top row center

Major seminary of the Marist priests - Lievelde, Holland
Ordination to the priesthood with six classmates
Fr. Ben Kasteel — first on left

A: Please help me understand some of the differences between formation as a diocesan priest and formation in a religious congregation.*

B: When you become a religious, you first make a novitiate, one or two years in seminary or community, followed by your first profession. I was twenty-one at the time of first profession, on September 12, 1958, and my family came to the seminary for this occasion. Usually about three years later the religious make their permanent profession.

As religious you are "professed." Professed means that you join a religious congregation officially, you make your vows of obedience, poverty and celibacy. Three vows of the religious. Sometimes also the vow of stability, meaning that if anything happened to the society, you are responsible to keep the society going.

After my first profession I entered the major seminary of the Marist priests in Lievelde, Holland, and studied two

---

*Religious congregations - institutes of consecrated life in the Catholic Church. These communities composed of laity and/or clergy (commonly referred to as "religious") take sacred vows to imitate Jesus more closely, primarily by observing chastity (celibacy), poverty, and obedience. Their members strive to live a common life following a religious rule or constitution under the leadership of a religious superior. Religious vows are to be distinguished from Holy Orders, the sacrament which bishops, priests, and deacons receive. Hence, members of religious congregations are not part of the hierarchy, unless they are also ordained priests or deacons (as is Fr. Ben). (Wikipedia)

years philosophy and four years theology. My ordination to the priesthood came on February 22, 1964, along with six classmates.

Many of the same courses are taught in seminaries, whether studying as religious or as diocesan. The main differences can be seen in the vows. Religious get ordained with the vow of poverty, celibacy and obedience. Obedience is vowed to the superior, who is in charge of groups as small as three, up to larger numbers as in a monastery. Diocesan priests vow obedience to the local bishop, and have no vow of community life.

For religious, the vow of community life often moves them far away from their family of origin. The community, in essence, becomes their nuclear family, committed to their care through retirement and death. Diocesan priests normally stay within their family context. Usually they go away to seminary, but return to the diocese where they grew up, and in retirement are cared for by their biological family.

Religious priests are always celibate, because it is essential to community life. As religious, the vow of celibacy is perhaps easier to follow because you have a whole support community around you. This is your family, you share things and function in life together. For diocesan priests, the vow of celibacy can be a very lonely reality. Often there can be support groups formed for diocesan priests, that come together monthly or so to share a meal, talk about what is going on in their lives. But here in Texas I call the priests who are assigned to remote parishes, without much priestly support around them, the "lonely rangers." I, too, was a "lonely ranger," not in Texas but in the Samoan Islands, but found support from the sisters that worked at the main station.

A: You have a really strong concept and experience of community. Even with this support around you, were there times of fear or uncertainty about the road of priesthood you had chosen?

B: Never. Not a moment. But you have to keep in mind that profession is not just saying you want to become a religious. Profession is that community accepts you. That community wants you, approves you to be a member. So it is a two-way movement. You not only say, "Well, I want to join the Marists." The Marists will say they want me, yes or no. Because the question will be behavior, will I fit into the group, will I be a liability or what will I be? So the religious community is also quite concerned about who the person is that they are accepting among them, because from there on you have to live with them.

A: Out of the three vows taken at your permanent

profession. . . poverty, celibacy and obedience. . . which one has been the hardest?

B: Poverty is not the hardest because you have all things in common, and the community is usually well taken care of. So poverty is, you don't own anything, you don't have anything yourself, it is not "your" car, it's the community car. Everything is community. There is actually a great freedom when you don't have to worry about all those "things." You are not collecting things for yourself. You are free from these worries.

However, I was a religious priest, now I am diocesan priest. . . now I have to think about how to take care of myself at the end of my life. If I had stayed Marist, they would have taken care of me, they would have put me in a facility they thought best for me, and I would not have worried over a dollar. Now I am responsible for myself. In my situation, not only is my family in Holland, but I have become an American citizen, so I will stay in America until I die. But I have to take care of myself, so I have to determine what I should worry about. . . and what I don't worry about I put in the hands of God, because I felt it was God's calling for me to change from religious to diocesan priest.

Obedience can be very difficult. You might be sent to a place or a ministry that maybe you think you're not capable of, but the superior wants to challenge you, wants to develop you. Today superiors are listening a bit more to the person, what the person wants. But officially in the religious communities the superior will decide where you go. For me, they decided to send me to the Samoan Islands, but they could have said I go to Fiji Islands or Solomon Islands. . . they could have sent me all over the place, I am just in their hands. I have no final say. I cannot say, "I am not going." This requires a great sense of surrender to God. . . it is not easy, but I have never regretted, and never looked back.

THE PARABLE OF THE SOWER.
When a large crowd gathered, with
people from one town after another
journeying to him, he spoke in a parable.
"A sower went out to sow his seed. And
as he sowed, some seed fell on the path
and was trampled, and the birds of the
sky ate it up. Some seed fell on rocky
ground, and when it grew, it withered for
lack of moisture. Some seed fell among
thorns, and the thorns grew with it and
choked it. And some seed fell on good
soil, and when it grew, it produced fruit
a hundredfold." After saying this, he
called out, "Whoever has ears to hear
ought to hear."

Luke 8:4-8

All three synoptic gospels contain the parable of
the Sower and the Seed. Perhaps this emphasizes its
importance for all students of scripture.

Certainly the audience of Jesus' day knew the
regularity of sowing and reaping, witnessing variable
results based upon conditions outside one's control.
But none would dispute, in that day or modern times,
the absolute necessity of *planting the seed*. The

promise of harvest perpetuates this pattern, our need to be sustained by the harvest motivates season after season of sowing. We simply must keep planting!

This parable most often focuses the success of harvest upon the condition of soil. Various types of soil determine the fate of the seed's germination. In a follower's life, receptivity of Jesus' words is determined by the type of "soil" one's heart possesses. Even as the seed (God's giving God's self) is coming forth from His divine initiative, our heart's receptivity is conditional upon the "soil" in which germination can take place. When the heart can understand, accept and hold fast to the transformation carried in the seed, then "fruit" will be produced. . . even abundantly.

Let's re-imagine ourselves, not as the soil but as the sowers, in light of St. Paul's truth that Christ lives within each believer. What if the seeds in this parable are the seeds of community which incubate from baptism, carried by each maturing disciple? What if, as the sowers, we hoard these seeds in a never-ending search for the "perfect" soil (right people, right priest, right music)? What if there were not a limited amount of seed, but an ever-replenishing supply of seeds to grow community, not just under Church roofs, but within homes, work spaces, neighborhood blocks? What if the sowers believe that no seeds are ever wasted, on any given day in any less-than-perfect soil? Indeed, what if the sowers trust that someday the harvest from casting will be bountiful, and cease the quest for gratifying results? What if the sowers, investing his/her seeds to produce community, relinquish rights to pre-assess soil conditions as worthy, or not, of the planting?

Amen, all ye sowers: we are planters of community. Within each of us are an infinite number of seedling communities. The planting soil is as close as the kitchen table, the house down the neighborhood street, the break room in the workplace, the gathering space of the parish. This makes us emissaries of Kingdom sprouts, commissioned to bloom where planted. But unlike this pilgrim priest, it could be argued that some of us are stowing away seeds, trying to disguise Christ's potential within us with false humility.

"Whoever has ears to hear ought to hear." Notice that Jesus called out to be heard, to reach those thinking, "I don't have enough faith to plant His seeds of community. The ones up front can do it."

This
Pilgrim
Priest

Charles Lascano, 6th Grade

media: graphite

"What inspired me to draw, and paint this design, was that I wanted to show how Msgr. Ben had been all around the world seeing lots of windmills, and to show that Msgr. Ben was a good priest."

49

CHAPTER THREE
Changing World

Being child number seven among twelve siblings,
Bennie knew the meaning of responsibility at an early
age. His older brothers, as well as his father, were
called away from the family farm to various labors
for the German army. During those years of Nazi
occupation in the Netherlands, lasting impressions were
forged on this child, many of which would serve him
well as a priest: resourcefulness, sense of community,
sensitivity to loss and injustice, and notably his
response in facing needs and limited options, "Oh yes, I
can do that."

During the years of nurture on the family farm,
Bennie was guided philosophically by his innovative
father, a man who sought out new ideas and integrated
progressive methods and technology. A peaceful man
who shunned conflict by finding good in all things,
Bennie's father would engage conversation during
meals around the latest agricultural magazine, soliciting
input from his sons and daughters alike. Theirs was
a small "mixed" farm which provided for their needs,
and allowed a marginal surplus of produce (potatoes,
corn, wheat) and livestock (cows, pigs, chickens) as a
source of income. Following the war years, the older
sons alternated time at neighboring farms as a means of

understanding, then implementing at home, alternative methods for increased productivity. These were the seeds sown for a budding visionary, a young man who would, by nature, be open to new perspectives, different solutions, varying interpretations.

Nowhere would these attributes be more tested than during his priestly years adjusting to the implementation of the Second Vatican Council. As a newly ordained priest in 1964, Fr. Ben was very aware of the ongoing council in Rome, convened by Pope John XXIII, finished and implemented by Pope Paul VI. Redefining church dogma during this decade of the sixties was fostered by the impact of post-World War II international initiatives. War had served as an ecumenical common ground, bringing Catholics alongside Protestants, Americans alongside Russians, paving the way for dialogue focused upon common objectives rather than dissimilarities. Whereas the First Vatican Council in the year 1870 had primarily focused upon the papacy, this modern council sought to redefine the roles of bishops, priest, and the laity, ultimately seeking a broader base of Catholic identity (evangelization) and emphasizing the college of bishops as successors to the college of Apostles (collegiality). As the familiar analogy describes, windows that had enclosed a musty, darkened inwardly-focused institution following the Reformation were now opened for light, fresh air, and gusts of wind that dislodged layers of sediment.

But in the early years of Vatican II changes, when Fr. Ben was an ardent young missionary priest in the Samoan Islands, chaos and uncertainty prevailed. In the midst of confusion, priests around the globe faced the difficult role of implementation and interpretation of change within parish and liturgical life. Equally disconcerting, priests themselves faced a shift in paradigm --- some of the absolute and essential teachings of seminary became fluid and reexamined. As Fr. Ben would later comment, "When the windows are opened, the force of the wind can blow around more things inside than one anticipated."

Fr. Ben Kasteel seated between father and mother
(all ten siblings attended ordination)
Note: an older brother already deceased

Presiding at first Mass in home parish
*Note: Pre-Vatican Council II liturgy required
consecration facing altar, the assembly behind the clergy*

A: Since the first Vatican Council defined more explicitly the papacy, it must have been very exciting to participate in changes that involved the priesthood. What were the early impacts of change on your ministry as a missionary priest in a distant third world country?

B: In the beginning, there was much confusion over translations from Latin to the vernacular. We had been taught in seminary that the essential formulas of the sacraments must be spoken in Latin to be valid. The official words and rituals of baptism, for instance, had been strictly enforced in Latin by the First Vatican Council, and anything else would be invalid. Now the question arose if the words of consecration could be translated, as it had always been mandated in Latin. So during Vatican II there was confusion because of the changes, and not knowing where it would all lead. Not even from one day to the next. Our bishop from the Samoan Islands had participated in the Second Vatican Council, so there was general acceptance of the changes we were asked to make. But for the older priest after all those years, to have the altars turned to face the congregation was quite an adjustment.

A: Did the changes of the Council happen all at once?

B: The last session of the Council began in September 1965, exactly one year after my ordination to the priesthood. All in all there were many different documents produced under two different Popes: a document on liturgy; document on the Church; a number of declarations on training of priests; the role of laypeople; mission activity of the church; ministry and life of the priests; on Catholic education; and relations between the Roman Catholic Church and other churches. During all the four sessions, everything the Council did was made very public by media and press, nothing was done in secret. But actual implementation began with fluctuations in the liturgy, which took place between 1965 and 1970. When I came to Samoa, one of my first assignments was to change the altar in all of the rural churches.

A: As newly ordained clergy with expectations of the priesthood, were the changes a difficult adjustment for you?

B: Because my dad had always been an advocate for change in matters of farming, I was not threatened by new ideas, new ways. And because Holland was, and still is, a progressive country, I was accustomed to accepting change. There had already been a movement in Holland to translate the Mass into Dutch language, and my dad embraced this, saying, "Oh yeah, now you know what's going on and we understand it." Also my community, the Society of Mary, had a great obedience to the Pope, so following his implementation was assumed. But it was hard to reconcile the former understandings, as in the practices of reverence around the altar, to be more open to the people. . . and as priests, to shift our understanding of our role between the laity and God.

It was helpful that our professors in the major seminary in Holland had been quite up to date. They had provided ways for us to study different theologians, more modern thought, particularly ones who brought a lot of scripture into theology. Even before the war, there had been a renewal in scripture study, and our awareness broadened as we discovered different sources in the Bible, different Biblical theology, historical research that helped us be open to a new way of thinking. Actually, the renewal of scripture in the Catholic Church had begun in the 1800's, as could be seen in official documents and encyclicals before Vatican II. So the scriptures were surely one of the major reasons why theology moved in a different direction.

THE PARABLE OF THE GOOD SAMARITAN.

But because he wished to justify himself, he said to Jesus, "And who is my neighbor?" Jesus replied, "A man fell victim to robbers as he went down from Jerusalem to Jericho. They stripped and beat him and went off leaving him half-dead. A priest happened to be going down that road, but when he saw him, he passed by on the opposite side. Likewise, a Levite came to the place, and when he saw him, he passed by on the opposite side.

But a Samaritan traveler who came upon him was moved with compassion at the sight. He approached the victim, poured oil and wine over his wounds and bandaged them. Then he lifted him up on his own animal, took him to an inn and cared for him. The next day he took out two silver coins and gave them to the innkeeper with the instruction, 'Take care of him. If you spend more than what I have given you, I shall repay you on my way back.'

Which of these three, in your opinion, was neighbor to the robbers' victim?" He answered, "The one who treated him with mercy." Jesus said to him, "Go and do likewise."

Luke 10:29-37

The style of teaching that Jesus preferred, the parable, required his audience to hear a story and walk away with an often puzzling conclusion. The characters and circumstances of the story frequently challenged long-standing perspectives, religious laws, and social mores of the time. It was up to each individual to ponder and internalize for oneself the "moral" of the story, and its subsequent application. Through the ages faith communities have repeated the stories in their own cultural context, facing and finding powerful revelations that breathe and grow alongside human experience. . . one of the many examples of scripture being the "living" word of God.

In light of the story's often surprising turn of events, the parable of the good Samaritan is no exception. No one listening to the Teacher would have guessed the Samaritan would be the hero of the story, and that subsequently they would face their own shortcomings as "good neighbors."

Yet another surprising take on this parable might be the following interpretation: what if the victim, injured and neglected on the side of the road, was an institution rather than an individual? What if a *system* was broken, and agents within the system walked by without heeding the evidence of suffering?

Within our Catholic Church history, there have indeed been transitory periods of an ailing institution, an example being the systemic obsession with authority following the proclamation of papal infallibility in 1870. Reformers would say that the distance between the Roman Curia and bishops, priests, and the faithful widened to the point of presuming the walls of the Vatican City contained the Church, reducing diocese across the globe to subordinate extensions of the hierarchy. Ironically, it was Pope John XXIII, an elderly, conservative pontiff chosen to fill the domineering shoes of Pius XII (1), who recognized the suffering victim as the Church in the late 1950's. Even his advisors were against his resolve to call the Second Vatican Council in 1962, the Council that ultimately moved the Church toward democracy and away from Italian-dominated politics (2). Further, this Council proclaimed the Church to be *all* the People of God, and that its mission applies "equally to the laity, religious and clergy" (Dogmatic Constitution of the Church, n. 30). Altar rails were removed, parish councils were established, the laity began to participate in the liturgy as lectors, cantors, etc., and the permanent diaconate was restored, just to name a few of the "bandages" applied toward recovery.

Enter a Marist priest whose vocational call spanned these historical developments. The reverence with which Fr. Ben speaks about Pope John XXIII is distinct, as if he witnessed the compassionate wisdom that moved this pontiff off the hierarchic highway of business-as-usual to rescue a "robbed people." Imagine this pontiff carrying the suffering servant to the inn, i.e., the Council that diagnosed the many wounds, while continuing to care for the victim. And finally imagine this priest from Holland, along with countless other clergy members, as the "innkeepers," in whose hands the pontiff placed the restoration process of continued healing.

The story does not end here. Rather, the story is still being written, with each of us playing a part in the narrative. The story will, most likely, include another Council in a period of history beyond our lifetime. Who will be the "good neighbor(s)" of the Third Vatican Council? Who will have the eyes to see and heart to respond, yet again, to the broken Body of Christ? Ours is a Church that has always been, and must continue to be, open to new embodiments of the apostolic message.

Sarah Settle, 6th Grade
Also Created Back Cover Design

media: watercolor; India ink

"I wanted to include all of Monsignor's life. I tried to draw a symbol from every place he has been."

CHAPTER FOUR

Samoan Initiation

Following seminary, ordination, and one year of
teaching in a minor seminary, Fr. Ben now stood on
the threshold of his childhood dream being realized.
The heart-strings once tugged by a missionary priest
now began their own melody. All the preparations of
school, spiritual growth, leadership skills and pastoral
training gave way to joyful, yet solemn, goodbyes
in anticipation of up to fourteen years away from
his native Holland. The time was June 1965; the
destination was the South Pacific Samoan Islands. . . a
culture, climate, language unlike any he had known in
his twenty-seven years.

There was never doubt about committing his
life at such an early age to this missionary path, and
everything possible had been done to prepare the
young priest for what lay ahead. But nothing short of
the experience itself could have equipped him for the
challenges to be found in this distant land. Such is the
hand of God on one's life. . . you are reassured knowing
the touch of the Master, learning to trust its strength just
at the time you realize you need it and not a moment
too soon!

First task at hand: cultural immersion. Before
arriving in Samoa, Fr. Ben spent time in Sydney,

Australia, considered the gateway to all Marist mission fields in the South Pacific. Here it was Ben's good fortune to spend time with a sick Samoan priest on leave, who taught him how to read Samoan, how to pronounce words. . . a "jump start" on the language which proved beneficial upon his arrival. But even with this advantage, Fr. Ben quickly discovered that the Samoans used three different versions of their language: a "high" language used for God; a "meeting" language; and a regular "conversation" language. The same word, used in any one of these levels, could mean something very different, depending on context. He also quickly learned there were cultural mores regarding when to speak. The Samoan people never talked to each other while walking. One sits down to carry on conversation, even in the middle of crossing a road.

There was little time for adaptation. Father Ben was assigned pastorship over seven geographically separated churches (each with two hundred or more parishioners), being sent out each Friday from a central station, traveling in a Jeep that had come from Holland. Pastoral responsibilities included baptisms, weddings, confessions, funerals at each location. . . and at the end of the day, wherever he was, presiding at Mass. Each of these seven parishes was served by local catechists, often couples, who were trained for administrative duties, even giving homilies. These catechists played an important role, softening the burden of unfamiliarity while the new young priest acclimated to his surroundings.

While Fr. Ben's spiritual and social engagements steadily progressed, the physical challenges of the islands rose exponentially. His first clue was in the bishop's car upon his arrival, when the bishop opened the console, pulled out a T-shirt, saying, "Hey, take your black shirt off. It is too hot over here. I have a T-shirt for you." From that brief initiation, Fr. Ben soon submitted to various necessary measures meant to promote good health: daily medication for "moo moo" (means "red") disease, a fever that can lead to delirium; boiling water for consumption; mindful selection of foods, preferably well cooked and without fly contamination; salt pills to compensate for profuse sweating and lack of fresh water; means to protect oneself from wild life, insects, and the elements when sleeping in open air.

Speaking of open. . . the culture of the Samoan Islands mandates that everything, *everything*, be conducted in the open. There are no secrets. All doors are open. Living with the natives means one gives up all claims to privacy. Every life activity is done in public view. This was not only an adjustment for Fr. Ben, but agencies such as the Peace Corp had difficulty preparing and maintaining staff within these parameters (or lack thereof).

It was not until after his arrival in Samoa that

the islands officially became a diocese. Father Ben arrived prior to this distinction, which meant that Rome (rather than the diocese) was directly responsible for management and fiscal support of this expanding community. Appeals for financial subsidy followed appropriate channels directly to the Holy See. The day came, however, when the diocese was established. . . and along with this "birthdate," autonomous underwriting. The missionary priests that pastored the region thus became more proficient at developing means of income for the impoverished parishes. One priest managed a lumber mill, others established farming initiatives.

Father Ben's particular passion led him to see and respond to educational needs of the children in his remote area. The pre-existing "elementary" school at the main station was supervised by women religious as a girls' school primarily focused on vocational skill training. Boys were more likely to learn trade skills as apprentices in on-the-job training around the community. Moreover, their rural youth population was educationally disadvantaged in that high schools only existed at the country's capital city. Few adolescents geographically separated from the country's capital could qualify for schools located at that distance. . . and unfortunately there were no other options at the time he arrived. So the vision of a local elementary school, simple yet purposeful for both boys and girls, was planted and realized in the rural township of Leulumoega.

This success naturally fueled the contagious enthusiasm of the new priest among his flock. His vision broadened to include a rural high school. . . again, simple yet pivotal, designed to further the scholastic development and skill training of both young men and women. The vision was well received, by both the townspeople and the bishop of the now-official diocese. All local hands were on deck to participate toward this goal, volunteering months of labor and personal resources to achieve their collective aspirations.

Fr. Ben farewell with father and mother
boarding plane for Samoan Islands
1965

Fr. Ben and the Women's Organization
Main Station, Samoan Islands

A: In the Samoan Islands, you were able to see firsthand the gap between western European nations and underdeveloped third world countries. What made the strongest impression on you?

B: There were so many issues the native people tolerated on a daily basis, but they never seemed to be bothered. Life for them was full of joy; they embraced me with hospitality and respect, and knew I had their best interests at heart. So when I proposed a much needed high school be built at the main station where I was located, the local people really threw their support behind the project.

A: So as a brand new priest on a first missionary assignment, you decided to take on a substantial project . . . building a school in a remote area of a Pacific island?

B: Yes, but remember that the high school was actually the second school project. We had already accomplished the first vision of adding an elementary school for boys. A very simple structure, but an accomplishment that convinced the people that by joining forces, good things could happen for all. So as discussion regarding a high school level building gathered support, it was considered totally possible, and as another opportunity to improve the future of the children from that region.

We had to have wood, so people from several surrounding main stations joined together to go to the top of a mountain and bring trees down. It was quite a commitment, cutting trees on top of the mountain and trying to slide them down, hauling some in a big truck. The project had gone on for about a year, collecting trees, so the resources and manual labor was piling up toward the peoples' dream coming true. Before we started, I had discussed the plans in detail with our Bishop Pio, and he had said, "Fine, no problem." So I was totally surprised when the Vicar General came to see me and said, "I come in the name of the bishop, and you have to stop work on the school."

A: You had already progressed one year on the building project and were told to stop? What reason did he give for this change of heart?

B: I remember saying to him, "I want to know the reason we are being told to stop, because these people have worked very hard, for a long time, to have these trees all around and now someone is saying, 'hey, stop.'" I felt that the people had a right to know, and I didn't want them to get mad at me, or blame the Church. I was insistent on knowing the reasons, and told the Vicar General I would go to the bishop to hear straight from him. He said, "You don't need to go to the bishop. The bishop is not explaining it to you. That's his job, his reasoning, and you just have to obey."

This was a real dilemma for me. First, I'm scared for my life with these people who have done all this work. I can't imagine myself announcing to the people that I am stopping this. I finally told the Vicar General that the bishop himself would have to tell the people, and that if I didn't get the reasons, then I'm leaving.

A: Oh my. What a beginning to your priesthood. How long had you been there?

B: This happened just at the beginning of the year 1970. I had been there for nearly five years. I decided that I was not good enough at this. I was so confused to have started a beautiful vision for the people, with the bishop's approval, then not to know a reason for it all to be stopped. So I did, in fact, tell the superior that I was leaving. I was sent to New Zealand.

In Auckland was a center for the Samoan missionaries, and it was there I had to really think about what I want to do now. My lifelong dream had been to go to the missions. I never thought about anything else. I had no desire to go back to live in the Netherlands.

There was an elderly German priest at this center that befriended me, knew I was struggling with a big decision.

He recommend to me that I go home for vacation, not to think about it too much, that the answer would come. So I went home. . . very unexpected, because when I left in 1965, I did not plan on going back for at least fourteen years.

I had been in the Netherlands less than a month when I received news from Samoa that Pope Paul IV would come to the islands. He would come to Samoa, he would visit the main station where I had been, and would dedicate the building of the future high school as a gift to the people in honor of his visit.

A: So did all the pieces come together with this news?

B: Yes. When our Samoan Bishop Pio had visited Rome, the plans for this papal trip to Samoa had been discussed. But when Rome does things, it's always under absolute secrecy. So the bishop was not allowed to say anything. Rome had put him under oath that he was not allowed to tell anyone that the Pope was coming to Samoa. That is why he could give no reason for stopping the school project. He stopped our work to delay the project just until the Pope could get there. And the Pope would donate the future school as a special gift of the Pope to the Samoans.

A: All of the questions about your vocational call led to

a moment of affirmation by the Pope himself!

B: I guess you could say that. It was very gratifying to know that the school would be built, and that all the work of the people would result in a beautiful reality. But by this time, I had already made plans to make another move. . . this time to the United States. The Marists had a very serious intention toward international exchange, to gather and implement cross-culture ideas and programming that would further their missionary efforts. So my future had been directed toward ministry innovations in a suburb of Cleveland, Ohio, to join what was already a Marist-led parish and become part of a team in training.

A: Does this mean you were never able to see the high school as a finished reality in Samoa?

B: Actually, I did return to Samoa, about two years later, by invitation of Bishop Pio. There were still two of my classmates from seminary on the islands, one brother and one priest. Bishop Pio wanted me to return to the islands and work with these two classmates to build a team ministry much like what was happening in Cleveland.

It was a difficult decision, because I loved my life at Pius X in Cleveland. I had become quite acclimated to the American lifestyle, the friendliness and good will, the food and climate being much less challenging than the conditions in Samoa. But I felt a kinship with these other two Marists, and decided to return in hopes of bringing this innovative team approach from Cleveland to help them further the island ministries.

This second time to the islands, the transition was even more challenging than the first. I had to accept again the limitations of travel, communication, climate and many more variables that were beyond my control or prediction. Nothing went according to plans. The two Marists I had returned to assist were both reassigned, leaving me isolated and in no hopes of a team-building ministry as projected.

It was a time of struggle. I had believed my vocational call to be a priest to the mission fields. What now? I was very fortunate that in Washington, D.C., our provincial headquarters well understood the conditions of the islands. This allowed for very open, honest discussion regarding my future, and the decision was made for my return to Cleveland.

THE PARABLE OF THE BARREN FIG TREE. And he told them this parable: "There once was a person who had a fig tree planted in his orchard, and when he came in search of fruit on it but found none, he said to the gardener, 'For three years now I have come in search of fruit on this fig tree but have found none. So cut it down. Why should it exhaust the soil?'

He said to him in reply, 'Sir, leave it for this year also, and I shall cultivate the ground around it and fertilize it; it may bear fruit in the future. If not you can cut it down.'"

Luke 13: 6-9

In this parable, Jesus uses a very common object to reveal a profound truth. The fig tree was the most valuable of all trees within the region, normally bearing fruit for up to ten months during a year. They were much more dependable than vines, and for that very reason were often planted among the vines to insure a harvest. It was also well understood by Jesus' audience that once planted as a seedling, it would take three years of maturation before the fig tree could be expected to produce fruit (3).

The story told by Jesus indicates that the required three years of initial growth had come and gone, and yet the tree had failed to produce. Many who hear the story focus upon the impatience of the master in wanting to do away with the unproductive tree, agreeing that the soil could be used for a more productive purpose. Assumedly, the parable portrays God as the master, Jesus as the vine dresser asking for more time, and the chosen people as the fig tree. . . established as a "seedling," expected to fulfill the divine purpose of the master, yet running out of time in bearing the fruit for which it was created.

For our purposes, please focus upon the tree itself, and be reminded that the tree had a great intrinsic value for which it existed. The tree was capable, by divine design, to reach an amazing potential for bearing fruit. The master knew this, and had waited accordingly for the maturation process leading up to actual harvest of fruit. And yet, the tree was not actualizing its potential to bear fruit. The tree was not being all the tree was created to be, even though all the necessary ingredients were already built into the tree by its very nature.

Those who have ears to hear would agree: the master justifiably expects the tree to be what it is created to be. But the compassionate vine dresser intervenes on behalf of the lethargic plant, convincing the master that in just a little more time, the tree will come around to accomplishing what it is designed to do. Both the master and the vine dresser know the tree's potential, know that everything is already inside the tree for it to be productive. The tree is singularly oblivious to the truth of what it is created to be ("oh, I am no fig tree, capable of bearing fruit. . . the fig trees are over there"). . . or is disobedient in some regard in following its divine design ("I am not quite ready to be all that I can be"). Consider the following quote regarding one's Christian potential:

> '. . . our deepest fear is not that we are inadequate. Our deepest fear is that we are powerful beyond measure. It is our light, not our darkness, that most frightens us.' We ask ourselves, Who am I to be brilliant, gorgeous, talented, fabulous? Actually, who are you not to be? You are a child of God. Your playing small doesn't serve the world. There's nothing enlightened about shrinking so that other people won't feel insecure around you. We are all meant to shine, as children do. We were born to make manifest the glory of God that is within us. It's not just in some of us; it's in everyone. And as we let our own light shine, we

unconsciously give other people permission to do the same. As we're liberated from our own fear, our presence automatically liberates others. (4)

Perhaps the parable of the fig tree can be understood as saying that obedience is not our submission to the demands and expectations placed on us by others, but rather obedience to the divine design to become all that we are created to be. And that sometimes we need trusted others ("Jesus with skin on") to help us see and accomplish all that we are created to be.

For those who profess vows and for the ordained, "vine dressers" become visible as superiors, bishops, provincials, and often the least among us (i.e., the leper for Saint Francis). For the laity, many priests, deacons, and religious teachers/directors are vine dressers as well, helping along the spiritual maturation process toward our bearing the fruit which we are, by design, capable of producing.

As a "fig tree" the best I can do is realize, first and foremost, my true and full divine design (according to Vatican II, priest, prophet and queen). . . then welcome the advocate role of the "vine dressers" in my life with full cooperation. In no time there should be evidence of buds on the branches.

This Pilgrim Priest

Sidney Herrera, 7th Grade

media: Prisma colored pencils

"What inspired me to draw this picture was his great adventure to follow God."

CHAPTER FIVE

Cleveland Collaboration

World War II had many effects on Fr. Ben's life,
both personal and communal. As Allied forces united
their efforts against Nazi Germany in the nineteen
thirties and forties, multinational dialogues regarding
military defense, political stability and human rights
were found mutually beneficial, extending well
beyond the war years. This collaboration of ideas and
languages profoundly influenced Fr. Ben's seminary
formation, as the Society of Mary (Marists) recruited
young men from beyond the seminary's Dutch
borders to enhance multicultural appreciation. In
daily seminary life, the language of conversation and
instruction would change from German, to French,
to English. . . all to promote familiarity with diverse
cultures. "International scholastics," a term used
frequently in our interviews, meant a cross-cultural
spectrum of curriculum that widened each seminarian's
perspective as he prepared for missionary fields around
the world.

This foundation served Fr. Ben well on his first
assignment to the Samoan Islands, and now would
find another multifaceted frontier in which to thrive
. . . the opportunity-laden melting pot of the United
States of America. As part of an international exchange

program, the Society of Mary sought locations across the globe, including the United States, in which to foster intercultural awareness. Priests assigned through this program found themselves "walking in the moccasins" of the faithful on the other side of the planet, often as learners as well as teachers.

So into this milieu of exchange, in July of 1971, came a questioning sojourner. "What does God have in store for me, an expectant priest with a heart for mission fields?" It did seem paradoxical that the journey was taking him from one extreme to the other . . . from far east to far west! More importantly, the path was moving the pilgrim from ministerial isolation to vocational teamwork. . . and the shift could not have been more timely.

Waiting for his arrival in a Cleveland suburban parish, heartland, U.S.A., was a support team of clergy and religious incorporating Vatican II changes within liturgy and parish life. Father Ben would become the fourth priest at the parish. . . what a far cry from his solitary, nomadic assignment in the southern Pacific islands! Weekly staff meetings divided responsibilities among pastors, providing for collaboration among partners. Shared insights within this diverse group fueled mutual zeal for Catholic faith rejuvenation, while common goals surfaced to form a framework in which all contributed according to their talents. Father Ben was identified as a gifted teacher of scripture, providing a much-needed catalyst to build confidence among the laity toward personal Bible study. In due time his passion for the people flourished in this team commitment to develop and implement Christ Renews His Parish, a weekend laity-led retreat for men, women and couples.

The spiritual tap root for this young sapling had found a deep spring of living water. This root would continue to anchor his subsequent assignments across the United States, as each new home would, within a year of his arrival, begin a series of Christ Renews His Parish retreats. The now-veteran pastor knew this to be the "tried and true" setting in which to access the heart of the people, and through which the people found the heart of their shepherd. He discovered that as laypeople got to know each other and felt more comfortable with their priest, involvement increased and a return to the sacraments was evident. Women shared their hearts, men shared their lives, couples shared their issues. . . all in the context of scripture and sacraments. Over and over, Fr. Ben saw vitality return to weary souls, and found his own strength renewed.

Two noteworthy team members at St. Pius X in Cleveland, Ohio, were religious sisters serving in various capacities on the pastor's staff. Sister Margaret Mack taught school and worked with pastoral programs in the parish. She became a close friend to Fr. Ben because her brother was a priest, and on many special occasions would take the young Dutchman to their family home when he had no other place to go. Sister Michaeline was Director of Religious Education and also served on numerous pastoral programs. She eventually took over the Bible study class that Fr. Ben had begun for parishioners. This support, both personal and in ministerial contexts, served to affirm his vocational call, as well as regenerate his morale. It also provided the framework that set a pattern for the rest of his ministry. . . recognizing and supporting the role of women in a wide variety of ministries within the Church.

By far the most significant acquaintance in Cleveland, which led to a lifelong friendship, was Fr. Eugene Driscoll, another associate pastor at St. Pius X. Father Gene, a one-year-ordained Marist priest, initially worked alongside Fr. Ben on a project to visit seventy homes of the parish to discuss changes in the Church since Vatican II. Together they attempted to clarify misconceptions and heal the hurts of unhappy parishioners. As Fr. Gene recalls, Fr. Ben had a wonderful way with people, and the many private conversations between the two of them about theology and ministry had a positive impact on his priestly formation. As years progressed, Fr. Gene became pastor of St. Pius X in Cleveland, and Fr. Ben would return from a second assignment in Samoa to become his assistant. Encouraged and passionate,

Fr. Ben worked primarily in developing and organizing Christ Renews His Parish weekend retreats, and also orchestrated the 25th anniversary celebration/dinner for St. Pius X parish. Neither of these dedicated disciples could have imagined their lives intertwined as God would have it, but as these memoirs are written some thirty-nine years later, their friendship continues to sustain their journeys and finds them only a short drive across town from one another (supping together most Saturday evenings). It seems fitting that in 2004, Pope John Paul II conferred the title Reverend Monsignor concurrently on these two champions building Christ's kingdom on earth.

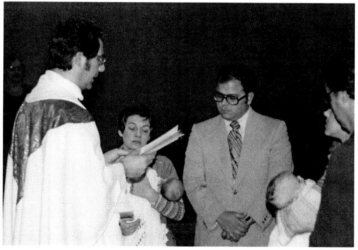

Sacrament of Baptism
St. Pius X in Cleveland, Ohio

Fr. Ben at parish gathering
St. Pius X in Cleveland, Ohio
1978

St. Pius X Parish
25th Anniversary Celebration
Fr. Gene Driscoll with his mother

A: Being sent to Cleveland, Ohio, came at a stage in your priesthood when there were some questions in your vocational journey. You had started something in Samoa, and it had been stopped without explanation, and you needed. . .

B: To be re-energized. I was looking for a new direction in my life, and had no idea what it would be. It just so happened that the Marist Society was very interested in an international exchange program, and turned out that I participated by following an assignment to the United States. The world was turning, so to speak, into an unprecedented arena of cultural integration following World War II, and Rome very much supported assimilation of different nationalities across the mission fields.

A: Did you have a preconceived idea of what the United States would be like?

B: My thinking was totally wrong about the United States. Totally wrong. From the time I had been studying as a novice, America was the country of the rich. It was the country of skyscrapers. It was a country of, what I would say, Hollywood vacation. So I had no idea that when I came to Cleveland I would find so many nationalities, all in the United States. Our parish had the Slovaks, the Polish, the Italians. . . any nationality you could think of from Europe was all there in that parish. And I met many people in the parish that had been in the war in Europe, flying over Holland, jumping down on Holland, lying behind farms in the bushes. It was a very welcoming community. They picked me up and I became part of them. In a very short time we became friends.

This friendliness was much more expressive than in Holland. In my country we did not shake hands when meeting someone for the first time. In United States, we shake hands every day, practically every time you greet each other. . . I still have to get used to that. But it is very good for me. Kind of getting away from the formality of Holland, where no one would get up from the table or take a plate away until everyone was finished. I had hardly ever been to restaurants to eat except on very special occasions before coming to Cleveland, and I sure was not looking for ice cubes in my drink.

A: So the United States surprised you with arms wide-opened. What other surprises were in store?

B: A totally new concept called team ministry. When I arrived at St. Pius X there were already three other priests, so my arrival there made three full time priests and one semi-retired priest. This was very new for me. For example, we would divide ourselves among different Bible study groups that were being held in homes of parishioners, each of us covering around four groups. The scripture study would come from booklets that would guide discussion, but at every meeting discussion would turn to renewal in the Church, things that were happening because of the changes evoked from Vatican II, people in favor and people against. Very lively discussion. I would be the "priestly presence," so to speak, because the people were just beginning to get in touch with the Bible and had so many questions. Eventually I started a Bible program that had twenty-five to thirty people attend for about a year.

A: Was this something new, for both you and the laity?

B: Yes, and I welcomed the opportunity, because during childhood my father had taught me to be open to change, that it often led to better ways of doing things.

A: But did the laypeople welcome the change?

B: At that time, the vast majority of Catholics were not comfortable with the Bible. Carrying one, reading one was unfamiliar because the Church had previously been more concerned that people would read the scriptures and be confused, not have enough understanding, not enough education. Vatican II implementations had just started when I arrived at Cleveland, so Bible study for the laity was a way of opening discussion as to the scriptural reasons for many of the Vatican II changes. Our Bible studies in parishioners' homes always ended with heartfelt discussion about changes in the Church, struggling to find the meaning behind what had been altered. And because the setting of these groups took place in homes, the priests had a chance to really get to know the people, their lives at work, in home, with family. This was tremendously life-giving for me. Often a family would invite me for dinner and they would invite a couple of their neighbors. We would spend the evening talking about everything that was happening "on the street."

A: The setting you have described sounds like an ideal relationship between laity and clergy. But this informal setting seems less likely the case in current parish life.

B: One reason for that is, again, due to Vatican II changes. In those days the laity and priests were not so organized into parish councils, commissions, finance, development and so on, because priests and sometimes staff were running the show. Nights were free for informal settings much more than the demands of monthly administrative meetings and follow-up events on active parishioners today.

But with the encouragement for laity to take ownership of their faith came the personal involvement and spirituality for which so many laypeople were hungry. For example, the Diocese of Cleveland began the program called Christ Renews His Parish. Before this program began, a retreat at the parish would be led by clergy or religious, speaking to or at the laity, and I suppose there was not enough connection. Christ Renews His Parish was a weekend retreat organized and led by laypeople with priests speaking in a minor role. As this program took hold at Pius X parish, you could really see what it meant to the people. Before they had come to Mass, been silent in church, left the church in silence, get in car with not much communication. Now there was a way to get to know each other, and for the priests to get to know the life of the people.

THE PARABLE OF THE YEAST.
He spoke to them another parable. "The
Kingdom of heaven is like yeast that
a woman took and mixed with three
measures of wheat flour until the whole
batch was leavened."

Matthew 13:33

Strange that Jesus would use this element, *yeast*, to describe the kingdom of heaven. Be reminded that throughout all of Hebrew history, every trace of yeast had to be removed from the house before the Passover Feast was celebrated. This Jewish understanding of yeast as symbolic of evil influence/corruption continues through all of New Testament scripture (5), <u>except in this parable</u>. Thus we find a shocking narrative to "wake up" an audience too complacent in their "pews."

Perhaps the point of Jesus' choice of words is found in the inherent attribute of yeast. . . it permeates all that it touches. Once mixed into a batch of dough, there is no stopping its effect upon the whole. This becomes the perfect parable to illustrate transformation of a parish community "stirred up" as participants in Christ Renews His Parish ministry.

I know this to be true, not just from the archives of Pius X in Cleveland, but through personal experience at Christ the King Cathedral in Lubbock. I was in the first leadership group for this laity-led retreat at our parish, when the women first "took and mixed" that sweet and Holy Inspiration that raises up everything it touches. Indeed, those gathered as leaders and participants found themselves enlarged from the inside out. I witnessed the "three measures of wheat flour" in the enormity of growth from women's retreats, to men's retreats, to couples' retreats over a period of nearly four years. In the process, "the whole batch was leavened" --- a community transformed from seeing their personal gifts as inconsequential, to claiming the spiritual treasury shared among us. We found our voices, our stories, could be a source of inspiration for others. We witnessed timid souls elevated by affirmation, and glimpsed the power of our true identity as priests, prophets and kings. We felt our reluctance melt away in the warmth of our pastor's encouragement, our former excuses of "I can't do that," evaporating like dew in sunlight.

Indeed, a flat, indifferent, unleavened gathering of parishioners can turn into something vibrant, delicious, life-giving. The ingredients were there all along. By following the recipe and resolve of the "chef de cuisine," our faith community found nourishment from our own hands. . . no renowned, degreed, flown-in speaker needed (although this is tasty, too!). Behold this abundance right in our midst, a sampler plate of the kingdom of heaven, where the feast is continually celebrated. Come to the table of plenty in your own parish hall.

THIS PILGRIM PRIEST

Brenna Lumongsud, 8th Grade

media: Prisma colored pencils

"I wanted to show the process of Msgr. Ben moving forward in his life towards the light of Christ. I wanted to show him starting with no knowledge of Christ, and moving toward the light with the knowledge of who Jesus is. Progressing from the darkness of ignorance to the shining light of knowledge and Christ."

CHAPTER SIX

Wheeling Blessings

Father Ben had gained so many positive experiences in Cleveland, Ohio, that his reassignment in June 1979, as pastor of St. Vincent de Paul in Wheeling, West Virginia, must have been bittersweet. This first pastorship came to the largest parish in the Diocese of Wheeling. . . a suburban parish with both a main church and a mission church, further enhanced with a parochial school. He was not the first Marist priest to be assigned to this parish, but as one esteemed Wheeling colleague recalls, Fr. Ben became one of their most beloved:

My name is Sister Joan Kreyenbuhl, CSJ. I was serving at St. Vincent de Paul as the parish DRE when Father Ben arrived, just one year after my own arrival. During that first year, in 1977, we had a visit from the Marist Provencial, who clearly told me there would be a major change coming to the parish that summer. I was certainly open to that, and encouraged that it would be someone open to Vatican II Church. My office was in the rectory, so I knew I would be affected by this new person. For this native West Virginian girl who had only spent one year out of my home state, the world was going to get a lot bigger. I found out that the new pastor was coming from St. Pius in Cleveland, but was really a native of Holland. . . the accent would be different from the Irish brogue to which I was accustomed in preceding pastors.

What I remember most from those early years was the surprise that I was suddenly being treated like an equal in what had been a male world. Almost at once my life changed and I was working from ten in the morning until ten at night. Every night there was a meeting. There was Parish Council and RCIA, Adult Education, Christ Renews His Parish, Evangelization, Outreach. Suddenly there were Parish Team Meetings bringing in the principal of the school along with the two associate priests. I don't think I had ever had a meeting with the former pastor, except the interview when I was hired for the position.

What Ben was able to do in me and in the parish as a whole was allow our gifts to be brought forward and used. Hundreds of people were involved in ministry, and I was organizing the details as Ben was creating the enthusiasm and the broader vision. We had become a team, gifts were called forward, and we were willing to work hard. The people were being fed and they were growing spiritually. . . they had met God, and discipleship was real.

Ben became more than a boss. He became a friend. I felt respected and loved by him. Occasionally I took him to my parents' home for a day away from the parish, and he established a close relationship with them as well. I especially remember his presence with them at my parents' fiftieth wedding anniversary, held at the little country church where they were married. Four months later my dad died. . . my mother passed away sixteen months after that. Ben was a support and concelebrated both of their funerals. Shortly thereafter he left Wheeling for sabbatical time in Rome.

*I had grown during those parish ministry years, and I knew I could do other things. My love for God flourished because of the love and acceptance I had received in working with Ben on his many projects. . . church renovations, school building, convent walls, rectory renovation, history writing in the parish, parish anniversary. I think this project is a **deja vu** experience . . . he is writing history once again.*

The challenges were many at this new assignment. With the help of Sr. Joan, as well as Sr. Margaret who had just become the school principal, there was much to accomplish at the school, convent, mission and primary churches. Perhaps the biggest detriment to parish life, as Fr. Ben had been informed, was the closing of steel mills and coal mines all across the surrounding area. The impact of lost jobs and a failing local economy turned Fr. Ben's focus upon pastoral and spiritual life opportunities to revitalize his new parish community.

Staff support at St. Vincent de Paul eagerly mirrored his resolve to fortify community. Sister Alicia, a very gifted musician, played "day and night" for all the funerals, weddings, liturgies and celebrations. She also served as bookkeeper for the parish, but his favorite memory is of the two of them singing together in the Ohio Valley Chorale. As noted above, Sr. Joan assisted in the continuous offerings of Christ Renews His Parish retreats for men, women, and couples for at least eight of the nine years Fr. Ben pastored in Wheeling. This programming became the basis for a tangible renewal among the laity. . . a real, vibrant and effective community experience that brought people back to Church, sparking enthusiasm to become involved.

And involvement led to renovations. Local business men and women offered their expertise and supervision to add a new wing on the school, replace windows, and make capital improvements to both church buildings. Father Ben was thriving in his first appointed pastorship just as he entered the height of mid-life, able to orchestrate a team of inspired staff alongside two assistant priests. The timing was right . . . there was plenty of work to be done and the people were ready for it. Directing Christ Renews His Parish for the first time, in collaboration with Sr. Joan, new music and more scripture was added to the program, a welcomed opportunity for Fr. Ben to take the lead in his own particular creative style.

But unlike his prior experience in Cleveland, the faith community in Wheeling dealt daily with the upheaval of economic uncertainties. Hard times had fallen upon the townspeople in the closing of all three coal mines. Many families accustomed to ample salaries lost everything. Some felt fortunate to find work at local chain restaurants, others attempted to start small business ventures on their own. It was Church that provided a venue to share the pain and bring together dialogue of hope. Christ Renews His Parish became an agent of healing, an open and honest reflection over the weekend of how God suffers with His people and will not abandon the destitute. Conversation centered around spirituality in practical terms. . . not just prayer that sustains the weary, but love of neighbor that leads to social service in action.

Perhaps this became the groundwork for Fr. Ben's expanding perspective on Eucharist. Here a people came together in community for two purposes --- a collective *thanksgiving* for the restoration of buildings and souls, and a collective *suffering* in response to economic conditions beyond their control. Thanksgiving and suffering: the two essential elements of Eucharist which must go hand-in-hand to understand the full presence of Christ.

Sr. Joan Kreyenbuhl, CSJ
St. Vincent de Paul School
Wheeling, West Virginia

St. Vincent de Paul School
Faculty and Administration

Sacrament of Confirmation
Fr. Ben at St. Vincent de Paul

St. Vincent de Paul
Wheeling, West Virginia

Leadership Training for Christ Renews His Parish
Couples' Retreat

Balloon send-off at Fr. Ben's farewell

A: How has the sacrament of Eucharist evolved during your forty-seven years in the priesthood?

B: Well, it has changed a lot since the day I was ordained. Our seminary training was prior to Vatican II changes, so the rite of Eucharist was very formal, reverent, in Latin . . . and as priest I had to be very aware of the punctuality of the ritual itself. Now the focus of this sacrament is on the meal of Jesus Christ, but as a beginning priest the focus was on the sacrificial offering, the "unbloody" offering of Christ to the Father. There were at that time two tables. . . one was the altar table where the unbloody sacrifice took place, and the other the communion table (or communion rail) where the meal was shared. Following Vatican II, the communion rail disappeared because the altar became the communion table.

Because the emphasis today is so much on the meal of Christ, I feel we have lost the important theology of the sacrifice so that sins may be forgiven. The sacrifice requires the action of consecration by the priest, using the symbols that Jesus instated when he said, "This is my body, this is my blood." The bread and wine become the sacrifice that Jesus made for the salvation of the world, and we then participate in that sacrificial action. There is so much more happening than just the sharing of a meal. That is why celebrating Mass is so essential in comparison to a communion service*. . . there is so much more going on than a meal. I really feel that there should be a combination of the focus prior to Vatican II and after Vatican II, so that the people never lose sight of the sacrifice. At every Mass we are still, through the sacrifice of Christ, offering up our sins, our failures, our brokenness. The Eucharist in THE celebration of the forgiveness of our sins.

A: Are you saying at the Eucharist we are invited to join with Jesus in offering up ourselves? Please say more about how we participate in His sacrifice.

B: In the moment of consecration there are two great elements. The element of the bread, the host, for the Jewish people would have been a reminder of God feeding them manna in the desert. It is a symbol of *thanksgiving to God* for all the blessing received, as individuals, as a parish, and as a worldwide community. Then there is the offering of the blood of Christ, which at consecration takes on the suffering of all humanity, the suffering of the world. Christ takes both of these elements, *thanksgiving and suffering*, and offers them to the Father. At Mass we are able to participate by uniting ourselves with Christ totally, loving and giving Himself to the Father for the salvation of humanity. Because the emphasis today is on being fed, we have lost the essence of there being two elements. We go to Eucharist to be nourished by the body AND blood, and often fail to see the invitation to

112

share the suffering. This is another reason why it is so important to perpetuate Mass as central to our faith. We have to focus on the transubstantiation of bread and wine, which after partaking becomes our transubstantiation. . . we become a people of thanksgiving, and we become a people who share in the suffering of the world. In communion service there is no partaking of the blood of Christ, only the bread of thanksgiving. . . it is, therefore, lacking in full participation.

When Jesus spoke the words at consecration, he didn't say, "This is bread and wine," he didn't say, "This is me." Jesus said, "This is my body which is given up," and I am united to this body within this community. Eucharist calls me, along with the entire faith community, to give up myself for the Church, for others, for the least among us.

A: This understanding of Eucharist, that the community members are united as the "body of Christ" being given up to the Father, certainly points out our connectedness to each other in this sacrament.

B: I never say, "I am the body of Christ." I feel much more comfortable saying, "We are the body of Christ." All of us together. And the great emphasis is on the love behind the sacrifice, especially found in the gospel of John where Jesus washes the feet of His disciples in a great act of selfless love. I like to think of this meal, the Eucharist, being like a real family meal, as something more special than just eating with friends. It should be at a family meal you express your blessings to each other, how important you are to each other, and also you carry each other, you carry each other's burdens and difficulties. As family you share the blessings, the thanksgiving for all you enjoy, along with the sufferings and pains, because you care about each other with a love that is deeper than friendship love. It is communion.

A: Do you try to lead others toward this deeper understanding of Eucharist?

B: Yes. But in many instances there is not enough adult education, so those who would like to gain more depth do not have the opportunity. So many of our parishioners are not seeking a deeper knowledge, but come to Eucharist once a week to "get credit." Most are content with a passive participation in liturgy, going through the motions, but without an understanding of meaning. I would like to see more active participation that combines body, mind, and spirit. Being physically present at Eucharist, knowing with your mind the meaning behind the words, actions and elements, and spiritually growing, being changed, by what is taking place. When a person believes that in the Eucharist one is united with Christ as the offering to the Father, then life is different during the rest of the day and week. Eucharist has to be followed by a life that is surrendered, that is no longer about "me," that is motivated by the love of Christ washing the disciples' feet. You don't just watch and go through the motions, you become what you are doing. . . the blessing and the sacrifice.

*Communion service - a Catholic liturgy that may be celebrated when no priest is available to celebrate Mass. It includes the readings of the day and the distribution of the Eucharist. However, it is NOT a Mass. Because a priest is not present, the prayers reserved to him are excluded, and there is no sacramental re-presentation of Christ's one Sacrifice on Calvary. Rather, previously consecrated hosts for Eucharist are taken from the tabernacle (the vessel for the exclusive reservation of the consecrated hosts) before the assembly recites the Our Father (The Lord's Prayer). (cuf.org - Catholics United for the Faith)

SAYINGS ON DISCIPLESHIP.

Great crowds were traveling with him, and he turned and addressed them, "If anyone comes to me without hating his father and mother, wife and children, brothers and sisters, and even his own life, he cannot be my disciple. Whoever does not carry his own cross and come after me cannot be my disciple. Which of you wishing to construct a tower does not first sit down and calculate the cost to see if there is enough for its completion? Otherwise, after laying the foundation and finding himself unable to finish the work the onlookers should laugh at him and say, 'This one began to build but did not have the resources to finish.'

Or what king marching into battle would not first sit down and decide whether with ten thousand troops he can successfully oppose another king advancing upon him with twenty thousand troops? But if not, while he is still far away, he will send a delegation to ask for peace terms. In the same way, everyone of you who does not renounce all his possessions cannot be my disciple."

Luke 14:25-33

116

This teaching on the costs of discipleship is not a contradiction to the love Jesus lived and professed. . . it is eyes to see His truth made manifest in and through His *disciples*.

Since first engaging this curious scripture I have wondered if Jesus really meant what he said. How can the Master teacher who lived and modeled unconditional love (even for enemies), now instruct his followers to hate their closest relations? How can the Son, who reframed the understanding of God from judge to Abba, Father, sound so harsh and demeaning of familial ties that bind? If one stays on the surface level with a literal interpretation of this teaching, the contradictions seem, at the least, confusing, and at the most, irreconcilable with the nature of Pure Love.

In light of Fr. Ben's powerful understanding of what transpires at each Eucharist meal, a fresh insight emerges that seems to alleviate the angst of this parable.

Consider that Jesus, St. Paul in his New Testament writings, and Fr. Ben are saying the same thing: the *disciple* sees himself/herself not confined by relational roles (father, mother, wife, child), but defined by incarnation truth ("I no longer live, but Christ lives in me"). It is not so much about doing away with people and/or possessions in one's life, as it is about identifying oneself as united with Christ. When this happens, roles, egos, personal agendas fall to the wayside in light of one's true identity. For the *disciple*, over-identification with roles (what I do) gives way to ecclesial truth (who I am). . . one is united with Christ, as invited at each Eucharist, to "do this in remembrance of me."

Since we are sacramentally united with Christ, we participate by carrying our cross during our physical time on earth. To "carry one's cross" means more than enduring the personal trials and tribulations of life circumstances. To "carry his own cross and come after me," means to leave the upper room (Eucharist) and participate in bearing the sins of the world. At each Eucharist meal the *disciple* accepts this invitation, to "carry one's cross and come after me," and this sacrifice, in unison with the entire faith community, calls me "to give up myself for the Church, for others, for the least among us," as stated earlier by Fr. Ben. This is where the rubber meets the road!

This truth does, indeed, require counting the costs and assessing the resources to follow through. Thanks be to God that "construction of the tower" or "marching into battle" was never intended to be brought about by individuals. When one counts the costs of being united with Christ, one sees all those gathered at the Eucharist table (past, present, and future) as the resource team to finish the building or to win the battle. The communion of saints is the ultimate stockpile for the Body of Christ on earth!

Noteworthy in this parable is the audience to whom Jesus addresses this truth. "Great crowds were traveling with him," i.e., these were *followers*. Jesus is pointing toward a deeper truth of <u>identity</u>. . . not just as intellectual or head believers, but as whole body, heart, and soul *disciples* who image His divine presence in the world. To realize oneself as His *disciple* implies a radical departure from normal routines and familial relationships. Stripping away the trappings of the ego, i.e., "renounce all his possessions," is a rigorous call to discipleship that Jesus issues to both male and female followers. . . an invitation to become the truth of who we already are.

Sophia Velasquez, 8th Grade

media: watercolor; India ink

"My painting was inspired by Monsignor Ben's spiritual journey It represents his past, present, and what is to come in the future. The windmills portray his background; where he comes from, and where he is now."

121

CHAPTER SEVEN
Sabbatical Discernment

The customary duration of a parish assignment for a Marist priest was six years. Father Ben had served as senior pastor at St. Vincent de Paul in Wheeling, West Virginia, for nine years, during which time the renovation of two church buildings and an additional wing on the parochial school had been completed. It was prudent to move on, and a Mass held outdoors celebrated the many blessings that had transpired during the pilgrim priest's tenure.

What came next?: a well deserved sabbatical year that included Christmas at his Netherlands family home. Father Ben had not been home for Christmas since leaving eighteen years earlier for the United States. This December 1988, was an opportunity for family and friends to welcome back the now world-traveled son who had followed the call to the mission fields.

That fall of 1988 was spent in Rome alongside other Marist priests, brothers, sisters, and mission sisters, coming from missionary locations across the globe. This was a glorious opportunity to consort with like-minded souls, sharing the ups and downs of cultural immersion, and the challenges of Kingdom work with minimal resources. Father Ben was particularly drawn to the men and women who had been serving in South America, and a seed was planted that ultimately blossomed into Hispanic ministry in Texas. But while in Rome, the focus was upon rejuvenating vision by probing history. . . particularly the roots of the Society of Mary (Marists). A sojourn in France, where the society was birthed, proved deeply insightful regarding the spirituality of the founders. If once-upon-a-time these men and women on sabbatical had vowed obedience to the Society of Mary, now was the time to recall and reaffirm the zeal and objectives they held in common.

Following Christmas, Fr. Ben left Europe for the second half of the sabbatical year (Spring 1989) in Santa Barbara, California. Here, an international school of spirituality allowed priests from far corners of the globe exposure to a myriad of presenters, mostly from the Diocese of Los Angeles. Topics ranged within the realms of Christian spirituality and theology, all illuminating current trends shaping the world's practice of faith. For the Dutchman who had a propensity to engage and exchange new thoughts, this was an ideal setting among peers and speakers, all of whom shared his openness to fresh insights.

This was also the time to seriously ponder his next placement within the options of Marist mission fields. Santa Barbara provided the milieu conducive for discernment, allowing time for prayer and reflection combined with stimulating input from human and scholastic resources. The seed planted in Rome by South American missionaries was being cultivated, the pastor once again eager to enter the field. Father Ben could see an entirely new context awaiting his pastoral skills, and from all that he heard in both Rome and Santa Barbara, the Hispanic culture was calling his name.

One interesting side note that transpired during this sabbatical year: at about the time Fr. Ben left his pastorship of St. Vincent de Paul in West Virginia, his name was placed on the list of potential Marist Provincial candidates in Washington, D.C. Knowing the election for the position would come during the fall, while he was away from the United States, meant trusting the cards to "fall where they will" in his absence. He placed this critical time of his priestly journey in God's hands, and remained on course to participate in the sabbatical program in Rome. Ultimately the other candidate won the election (narrowly), resulting in Fr. Ben's availability to be assigned to further pastoral positions. How would this pilgrim's journey have been different had he taken "campaign" matters into his own hands? This is a primary example of reasons to follow this shepherd's guidance. . . God can be trusted with outcomes: our part is to participate when called upon for the greater good. In this case, the greater good was in a struggling parish in West Texas.

On sabbatical in Santa Barbara, California • Spring 1989
International gathering of priests studying spirituality
Fr. Ben in sunglasses close to center

A: How did your sabbatical year in Rome and Santa Barbara fit into the whole spectrum of your priestly vocation?

B: It was a great year to, first of all, be away from all activity. During this time you catch your breath and rest well. Also a good time for reflection upon all the things you have become involved in, what has been most life-giving, what most frustrating, how is God moving, and so on. It is also a kind of preparing for the future. . . what is next, what you want to do different or do the same. To come together with sisters and brothers serving God in different ministries all over the world brings new perspective for the future.

A: Did this year away from priestly responsibilities reframe your motivations, your goals, in any way?

B: I think what became clear was being able to see the enrichment of going from culture to culture. . . from Holland to the South Pacific to the United States. . . and what that means to you. When I met all these priests and nuns on sabbatical, who worked in all different parts of the world, I knew I wanted to continue to be a missionary. It was this experience that strengthened my desire to go to the Mexicans, the Hispanics.

A: There was yet another new frontier?

B: That's right. Because the Marists were always talking about it. I was in the leadership of the Marists at this point, and all the time we were saying we should be going to the Hispanics. There was lots of talk, talk, talk. I am not one of talk. I like to do. So that is the reason I decided I wanted to go to Hispanic ministry. And I don't think too much, well, I have to learn Spanish or whatnot . . . just go. God will provide.

A: How did the theological and spiritual studies during your sabbatical better prepare you for Hispanic ministry?

B: I would say the program, particularly in Santa Barbara, was very helpful in training us to solve things pastorally. Because there is a big difference between having rules, these and these rules, on paper, and the practicality of solving issues as they arise. Say if you have a couple that cannot get their marriage nullified, how do you deal with it? So we had a very good canon lawyer helping us understand the rules while acknowledging the circumstances. That's what I really liked about the program, the focus on how to solve things pastorally. Since there were participants from different places and backgrounds, it was a great moment of sharing how to, practically, deal with the needs of the people.

A: What is it about Marist spirituality that continues

to ground your skills in dealing with the needs of the people?

B: We spent a lot of time during the sabbatical year being reminded of the precepts that founded the Society of Mary. To say, in summary, what it is about Mary, and about the Holy Family, that the society seeks to perpetuate in the mission fields. Their focus in spirituality is to look at Nazareth. . . the spirit of Nazareth.

A: The spirit of Nazareth? The town of Nazareth?

B: Yes. The town of Nazareth, where the Holy Family lived, where Jesus grew up. The major attributes found in this setting, during these years, the family was hidden and unknown. Like Mary, simple. Like Mary, very hidden in the early Church, not the big leader, just simple, participating in evangelization without a lot of attention. Our society perpetuates the spirit of Nazareth in this way. . . never seeking honors or advancements for ourselves, all things done in a spirit of humility. Our founders in France thought that, like the Jesuits focused on Jesus, we would focus on Mary, and upon bringing Mary's spirit to work in the Church. We were never taught to aspire to titles or recognition. We try to think and to act as Mary would, from a place of utter humility.

A: So during the sabbatical year you found clarity about your next "hidden and unknown" setting? And it was toward the Hispanic culture?

B: That is evident in my devotion to Our Lady of Guadalupe. Mary came to the most hidden, the most humble person she could find, Juan Diego, to reveal her presence and compassion. In this most obscure place, Mary can be found. Within the most humble hearts she resides. It is upon these precepts that I was formed in my priestly vocation and they have never ceased to sustain me. Just like Joseph stood in the background, in constant support of the plan of God for the world, I hope to participate from behind. I would like my legacy to say I was a quiet man who never wavered.

PARABLE OF GUESTS INVITED TO FEAST. He told a parable to those who had been invited, noticing how they were choosing the places of honor at the table. "When you are invited by someone to a wedding banquet, do not recline at table in the place of honor. A more distinguished guest than you may have been invited by him, and the host who invited both of you may approach you and say, 'Give your place to this man,' and then you would proceed with embarrassment to take the lowest place. Rather, when you are invited, go and take the lowest place so that when the host comes to you he may say, 'My friend, move up to a higher position.' Then you will enjoy the esteem of your companions at the table. For everyone who exalts himself will be humbled, but the one who humbles himself will be exalted."

Then he said to the host who invited him, "When you hold a lunch or dinner, do not invite your friends or your brothers or your relatives or your wealthy neighbors, in case they may invite you back and you have repayment. Rather, when you hold a banquet, invite the poor, the crippled, the lame, the blind; blessed indeed

will you be because of their inability to
repay you. For you will be repaid at the
resurrection of the righteous."

    This parable, using host and guests, resonates
beautifully with Fr. Ben's depiction of the "spirit
of Nazareth." In their modesty, the Holy Family
patterned for us the attribute of humility often referred
to as "Christ-likeness," and a multitude of models in
Christian faith have followed suit. A prime example
is Mother Teresa, who refused to be present to accept
the Noble Peace Prize. She preferred the "lowest
place" in the slums of Calcutta and left the spotlight for
dignitaries and "more distinguished guests."

    How does one overcome the allure of the ego which
seeks the "place of honor"?

    Perhaps the second part of the parable holds a
clue. Jesus is directing our attention toward a venue in
which to learn how to overcome the ego. It is a social
occasion, one of gaiety and repose, around food and
drink that one is providing for the joy of fellowship
with others. It is the "others" in this story that makes
it a parable. . . for a parable is meant to change the
way one perceives truth. In this parable of hosting a

banquet, one begins with the norm of inviting friends, relatives, and wealthy neighbors to the feast. Most readers, having held such gatherings around their dining tables, can identify with this first guest list.

But it is not in our normal, accustomed, familiar settings that we find the blessedness of humility. Rather, it is when we seek the low and hidden "others," around which to hold a banquet; it is when we bestow hospitality, sustenance, and even our undivided attention to their "other than" presence in our midst.

In this context we become *unlearners,* and take steps toward emptying ourselves of personal agendas (i.e., the need to be repaid). The poor, crippled, lame and blind become our *unteachers*, and their powerlessness becomes our blessing. In this surprising context, the pursuit to climb *and be seen* is redirected toward the potential to descend *with those hidden. . .* just as the Marist founders envisioned for their Society of Mary.

And Mary would be the exemplary model on which to sustain this vision of "hidden and unknown" Marist spirituality. In her unique life and role as Mother of God, we see the one who was empty of all egotism, and the more she received God, even through suffering, the more she became hidden in God. Even though we honor her in countless visible ways, Thomas Merton so aptly writes about the hidden Mary:

It is because she is, of all the saints, the most
perfectly poor and the most perfectly hidden,
the one who has absolutely nothing whatever
that she attempts to possess as her own, that she
can most fully communicate to the rest of us the
grace of the infinitely selfless God. And we will
most truly possess Him when we have emptied
ourselves and become poor and hidden as she is,
resembling Him by resembling her. (6)

Merton goes further to illustrate what I believe to be
a striking correlation with Marist spirituality of "hidden
and unknown:"

It is a tremendous grace, then, and a great
privilege when a person living in the world we
have to live in suddenly loses his interest in
the things that absorb that world, and discovers
in his own soul an appetite for poverty and
solitude.
. . . To seek this emptiness is true devotion to
the Mother of God. To find it is to find her. And
to be hidden in its depths is to be full of God as
she is full of Him, and to share her mission of
bringing Him to all men. (7)

Whatever one's current state of internal affairs,
there is always more of which to let go. The men
ordained as priests and deacons, the women and men
vowed to religious life, would be the first to confirm

this. In God's time, with Mary's intercession, and upon one's choice to relinquish the "place of honor," we all have opportunities to find the hidden places of transformation.

THIS PILGRIM PRIEST

Joseph Marzak

Joseph Marzak, 7th Grade

media: Prisma colored pencils

"My painting was inspired by all the different places Msgr. Ben has been in the past and where he has ended up. The old windmill represents Msgr. Ben's travels, and the new modern windmill represents Lubbock."

137

CHAPTER EIGHT
Plains Frontier

Again the winds of the Spirit blow as they will, shifting tides, surfacing desires in the heart of the pilgrim priest for yet another fresh beginning, in yet a totally new context.

The Marist community, being focused upon missionary fields and international diversity, was eager to develop their presence in growing Hispanic populations within the United States. This provided the perfect fit for Fr. Ben's new assignment. . . warm climate, rural setting, new cultural experience. He found an accomplice in his longtime friend and fellow Marist priest, Fr. Gene Driscoll, who at the time was completing his role as Marist Provincial in Washington, D.C. Together they considered the options of Brownsville, El Paso, and Lubbock, Texas, both of them looking for a quiet place to utilize pastoral skills. By process of elimination (Brownsville too hot, El Paso too big), the Diocese of Lubbock became their destination. In June 1989, following an intensive three-week Spanish language program in Mexico, Fr. Ben was assigned to the neighboring parishes of Matador, Paducah and Floydada, while Fr. Gene took the senior pastor position at Sacred Heart parish in Plainview. This seemed a pleasing, comfortable beginning for both.

Father Ben had just completed a sabbatical year of travel and spiritual renewal when this new assignment was formulated. He voiced one particular goal to his superiors as he re-entered active ministry: "I don't want to go anyplace that I have to build a school or church. Just let me go to the country, a missionary area with few needs other than pastoral leadership." These three rural towns fit that description, but the winds of the Spirit unveiled an urgent need for capital improvements just down the road, and Fr. Ben was reassigned after just one week.

The structural demise of Our Lady of Guadalupe parish in Plainview had been ongoing, reaching a critical stage just as the two Marist priests arrived in the diocese. The original church building, built in the barrios for the Hispanic population it served, suffered the effects of the flood zone in which it stood, with a collapsing floor that was quickly becoming a liability risk. Rather than construct a new foundation above the flood plain in an effort to restore the building, Fr. Ben worked in collaboration with Bishop Michael Sheehan to begin the arduous task of relocating the parish. With limited resources, both in choices of existing buildings and in capital outlay for the moving project, Deacon Ramos approached Fr. Ben with a timely proposition, "We should have a look at that bank building that is empty. It looks good for a church." To which Fr. Ben replied, "We are never going into a bank building. That is the last thing we should consider."

Never say "never." Several weeks later, having
exhausted options of other buildings and storefronts
in Plainview, a group that included Fr. Ben, Deacon
Ramos and a dozen parishioners spent a Sunday
afternoon inside that empty bank building. . . and the
rest of the story became a beautiful chapter in the life
of Our Lady of Guadalupe community. Negotiations
reduced the asking price, but this low-income parish
still had a massive monetary hill to climb --- all the
more reason Fr. Ben fell in love with the Hispanic
populace of this community. Their spirits consolidated
around their love of Church as the center of life,
evoking the impetus to see fundraising as a celebration
of sorts. Three events provided seed money while
volunteered labor ensued on the interior revisions.
Within nine months of signing the contract, the
bank-turned-church was remodeled and occupied in
September 1991. Father Ben's rectory was inside what
had been the bank vault.

Did Fr. Ben get what he wished for in his new
assignment? Contrary to the fact that, indeed,
another building project was undertaken, everything
he imagined in this new cultural setting did come to
pass. He was embraced by a warm, willing, familial
community that led him into their big Hispanic hearts,
and he in turn led the way through plans, negotiations,
and financing to see their collective dream come true.

Had it not been for the "dreaded" building scenario, Fr. Ben might not have recognized so quickly the spirit of the people he now shepherded. It was a case of mutual affection, and to this day, Fr. Ben speaks with immense gratitude of his time as pastor of Our Lady of Guadalupe, Plainview, Texas.

NOTE: During this segment of the pilgrim's journey, the Diocese of Lubbock was assigned their second bishop in June 1994. Arriving from Chicago, Illinois, to assume this position, Bishop Placido Rodriguez would become a valued friend and trusted superior to the Marist priest. Under this bishop's leadership, Fr. Ben would serve as Vicar General of the Diocese of Lubbock, ex-officio member of the Presbyteral Council, Personnel Board, Finance Council, Building Committee, and the Bishop's Pastoral Team. Within the swelling diocesan responsibilities, Fr. Ben was incardinated into the Diocese of Lubbock on May 22, 1997. Becoming a diocesan priest, thirty-nine years after being professed a Marist, was choosing allegiance to and remainder of life within the Diocese of Lubbock. Inside our geographical region this pilgrim will someday retire, our honor in being his chosen home-based community.

Our Lady of Guadalupe Catholic Church
(former bank building)
Plainview, Texas

Fr. Ben in Hispanic headdress - farewell celebration

Our Lady of Guadalupe parishoners' gift
Fr. Ben with sombrero
(Pictured with Bishop Placido Rodriguez)

Women's group who prepared meals after Sunday Masses
for Our Lady of Guadalupe

A: I know that there have been countless times in your priesthood that you have known for sure that you made the right commitment, you took the vows, you were on the right path, you were doing God's will. Tell me a time when you were absolutely sure you had done the wrong thing.

B: I have never thought that. Never. Anytime in my life I had to do it over, yes, I would. Yes. Probably because my ministry has always been very enjoyable, very satisfying, very meaningful. I always felt enormous appreciation from the people.

A: From, or for?

B: From the people. Yes. The people have always had an extremely grateful spirit every place where I have ever served. Not just on a fair weather day, but on a continual basis, the people have shown a lot of gratitude. When I was in the islands visiting the different places and making a lot of effort, the people were appreciative because some priests wouldn't make that much effort. So I like to give good service. People have always been extremely grateful, that's what I feel. And their gratefulness has been extremely gratifying.

A: I suspect that not all of your colleagues would answer as affirmatively as you have. If you could counsel seminarians, how would you prepare them for the range of response during their years in the priesthood?

B: I think that a priest who doesn't preach well, the people of the parish might be very happy with him because he's a great friend. Each priest has his own quality, and overall this represents a range of giftedness. One can be a great teacher, one is more pastoral. . . you find a great variety. If you are not appreciated in one area, they will appreciate you in another area. I think it is only when you are extremely naive as a priest, and you come in and start to dominate everything, maybe without even recognizing it, you will create a lot of problems. And you get your own punishment.

A: An interesting observation. Please say more.

B: There are times when a priest enters a new assignment with what I would call "narrow-mindedness." The new priest might not have a clue of the place itself, comes in, and tries to put everything according to his likeness. This failure to listen creates a lack of understanding of the history and programs already in place, many of which the people themselves started years before.

It has been better for me to spend time observing the way things are when I arrive, then in a timely way, guide the future. This is especially true when a priest enters a culture different than his own. Only a very narrow, unteachable person would not allow the people to tell you about their customs. Then you understand things are much deeper than what is being seen. . . there is a depth of mentality, a spirit of the people behind the actions and practices. You have to be open, trying to understand the unique personality of each parish. If you are even a little bit open to learn things you didn't know before, there are so many teachable moments. Maybe because my dad always wanted to know the latest thing, always liked to see what is new, this has been one of my greatest privileges as a priest.

A: Not only have you used a variety of pastoral skills in different countries, but you have also developed a broader perspective of the priesthood from four decades in ministry. How is today's parish different from your early assignments?

B: First of all, when I began my ministry in the islands, I came from seminary training in theology, scripture, languages, canon law, etc. Then I was sent to a mission field where all of that was not enough, because real life was happening with these people, and now I had to deal with real life and a lot of complications. I have always felt that the laity became my teachers, then and now. I have learned an enormous amount of theology, spirituality, team skills and implementation from the laity. Some younger priests in today's world are threatened by a well-informed laity, and this is more and more the case. Not just educated, but talented, trained, specialized. This has a tremendous impact on the life of a church, when the priest does not have to do everything himself, but has qualified parishioners, sometimes on staff but mostly volunteers, to enhance daily operations and inform the future vision. Even in smaller parishes the laity is full of faith and optimism that can teach the pastor how to persevere, get things done. Each parish offers the priest the chance to learn, adapt and grow along with the laity . . . and that can be the most rewarding experience in the priesthood.

A: Has there been a re-evaluation of the commitment you made as a young man, a validation of the sacrifices within priesthood, such as celibacy?

B: I have a strong sense of gratitude knowing that God has helped me through certain moments. Moments when, like Mary, you are being asked to participate, dedicate yourself more consciously, and feel that God touches you. . . similar to the growing intimacy in a marriage commitment. The priesthood has always been the dearest to me, the most valuable way of knowing who I am, what I am doing, what my life is about. And celibacy has allowed me to grow in this intimacy, giving me opportunities to deepen my spirituality, having solitude and so on. I never have to worry about providing for or neglecting a family, or having family obligations interfere with my role as priest to the people.

A: So can you say that within the priesthood you have found the blessings, fulfillment, and growth of covenant love?

B: Absolutely. Absolutely yes. If you just think about

Saturday confessions, the priest tells the person that their lives, their mistakes are forgiven, wiped away before God. . . and you see that person with new courage to continue their journey. This creates enormous joy for me . . . for I know how pleasing it is to God. And also very holy moments of anointing of the sick, to see a person becoming calm, how they feel at peace. It is how you feel very satisfied when doing things for your children. In the same way, as priest you feel what it really means in the life of the people.

Also for me, the Mass itself becomes more valuable each day. All the suffering Jesus was willing to carry in the spirit of love, Jesus offering Himself to God, that is offered each Mass. . . and it is a moment in which I become so grateful. When I lift up the bread, in my mind I see all the blessings that people receive in their lives from coming to Christ. And when I offer the blood of Christ, I really pray for all the suffering that is in the lives of people. As priest you get so much to pray about! People are really hurting, and I think as priest, it is a privilege to have so much opportunity to pray to bring people close to God and His glory. So I feel that priestly life is very satisfying. . . and cannot imagine for myself any higher form of covenant love.

A: In a word or phrase, what has been your "mantra" as a priest over all these many years, that has been suitable regardless of where and when you served as pastor?

B: I remember in Wheeling, West Virginia, that they laughed and teased me about the first thing I said when I arrived. . . but it was true then, and still is. "I am Ben. I have come to make you happy."

THE PARABLE OF THE PERSISTENT WIDOW. Then he told them a parable about the necessity for them to pray always without becoming weary. He said, "There was a judge in a certain town who neither feared God nor respected any human being. And a widow in that town used to come to him and say, 'Render a just decision for me against my adversary.' For a long time the judge was unwilling, but eventually he thought, 'While it is true that I neither fear God nor respect any human being, because this widow keeps bothering me I shall deliver a just decision for her lest she finally come and strike me.'"

The Lord said, "Pay attention to what the dishonest judge says. Will not God then secure the rights of his chosen ones who call out to him day and night? Will he be slow to answer them? I tell you, he will see to it that justice is done for them speedily. But when the Son of Man comes, will he find faith on earth?"

Luke 18:1-10

During the course of our taped interviews, recording the events and reflections of Fr. Ben's life, I asked what was the hardest part about being a priest. I fully expected the answer to be about raising money for capital campaigns, or about the physical/emotional/ spiritual demands of pastoring a large parish without an assistant priest, or about the isolation of priestly life. So I was surprised, as you may be, by his answer.

He said the hardest part was asking the parish to dream dreams, imagine the best community experiences to be found, step forward as owners and leaders of programming. . . then as pastor to decide which of those visions should move forward, and which should not be pursued. To say "no" was the hardest part.

I remember my stunned reaction. This seemed so miniscule compared to the largeness of buildings being completed, or to the seriousness of the shortage in priesthood vocations. But his answer forever changed my idea of genuine priesthood leadership. At the end of the day, it is not about bricks and mortar, it is about building people.

Father Ben went on to elaborate the process of

discernment required weekly, sometimes daily, in the life of a parish priest. Do the resources exist to allow a reasonable chance of success? How many lives will be touched by this program? What priorities in community life are being met by this undertaking? Accordingly he explained it can become disheartening for a priest, in light of the number of books being published about model parishes and programming, to acknowledge that implementation in the field is not as easy as presented. Even a sense of guilt can plague the senior pastor who must reserve his own energy, as well as parish resources, to do selected things well, as opposed to many things moderately.

What a responsibility to carry on one's shoulders! Surely this points to some advantages of team ministry, parish and diocesan councils, where burdens of discernment, decisions, and implementation are shared among the faithful.

And now we make connection between decision making and the parable of the persistent widow. It is no accident that this New Testament story depicts a woman's voice that will not be silenced (*Sophia* in Greek), an ageless voice carried through human vessels, sometimes those with authority, sometimes those completely powerless (the widow). It is *Wisdom* that raises her insistent request. . . *Wisdom* recognized

by Old Testament kings to be valued above all other
blessings, described as the first-born of creation (8).

> *Wisdom cries aloud in the street, in the open*
> *squares she raises her voice; Down the crowded*
> *ways she calls out, at the city gates she utters*
> *her words. . .*
>
> *Proverbs 1:20-21*

How does Fr. Ben's answer share meaning with this
parable? That *Wisdom* will speak through the events
of the world and catalysts in parish life to precipitate
change, impact decisions, alter courses of action.
Namely, that *Wisdom* can be counted upon, will not
remain silent, in the midst of leadership discernment.
As members of the hierarchy carry the final authority
(as does the judge in the parable), they can be confident
that visionary proposals coming from *Wisdom* will not
be deterred and will continue to manifest themselves as
even a persistent annoyance. Less worthy or untimely
initiatives will fade away under resistance. The
"judge" will ultimately know the difference and rule
accordingly.

We might pray this scripture on behalf of Fr. Ben
and all priests who seek *Wisdom*:

He who fears the Lord will do this; he who is
practiced in the law will come to wisdom.
Motherlike she will meet him, like a young bride
she will embrace him,
Nourish him with the bread of understanding,
and give him the water of learning to drink.
He will lean upon her and not fall, he will trust
in her and not be put to shame.
She will exalt him above his fellows; in the
assembly she will make him eloquent.

Sirach 15:1-5

As faith communities share responsibility for the future of our parishes, those involved in discernment need not solely rely upon themselves, but rather place every confidence in our faithful God who has counsel in store for the upright. This very legacy undergirds our priesthood, the men among us who carry His counsel. . . sometimes by saying "no." Through their discernment, our collective dreams will unfold, and *Wisdom* will have her way.

Elena Luera, 6th Grade

media: watercolor; India ink

"Looking at some wooden shoes inspired me. Monsignor Ben is Dutch so that also inspired me. His devotion to God made me think I should put a cross on the shoes. That is where it all came together."

157

CHAPTER NINE

Darkness And Light

From his room without a view in Plainview. . . what was previously the vault within the bank building. . . Fr. Ben enjoyed a comfortable abode right in the center of parish life. His pastoral instincts found this advantageous, to keep an eye on things and have quick, easy access to the people of Our Lady of Guadalupe, as well as programming venues within the church facility. It was "nice and quiet," thick steel walls insulating him from outside noise (including fire trucks next door!). He was altogether content when Bishop Placido Rodriguez first approached him about reassignment to Christ the King Cathedral in Lubbock, Texas.

Much transition had been taking place at the cathedral parish, somewhat removed from Fr. Ben's life in Plainview. Bishop Rodriguez explained that the senior pastor, Msgr. James Comiskey, was due to retire following twenty years of service at Christ the King. He further chronicled the status of partially complete renovations and expansion of the cathedral space which would prove a factor in this new assignment. The bishop reasoned these transitions needed guidance from a well-seasoned, competent shepherd's hand.

Thus, history records Fr. Ben becoming the fifth pastor of Christ the King parish, the second Rector of Christ the King Cathedral. Confident that God would finish the good work He had begun in the nearly completed renovations to the sanctuary, the pilgrim set forth on perhaps his final sojourn. He began this post undaunted by the expanded administrative duties, including parish, school and diocesan committees of all kinds, not to mention the challenges inherent in finishing a project begun under former governance, and under the looming clouds of sexual scandal among the priesthood.

As previously noted in both his personal and spiritual approach, Fr. Ben entered the cathedral environment intent on listening. Quietly he made the rounds, seeking exposure to leadership already in place, the mood of the people, the programming underway, the operative format of parish council. Observe, listen, pray, more listening. . . what is not being said? What is the "pulse" of the people? Where are the foundations upon which to build? Where are the "wounds" upon which to apply ointment? How can opportunities for spiritual growth be introduced? Assessment of resources --- spiritual, financial, emotional, human (within staff and lay leadership) --- all needed to be seen with fresh insights.

During the mid-nineties, prior to Fr. Ben's arrival, executive decisions had been made that affected future vision and plans for the cathedral's parochial school. Consensus had determined financial support for the school to be increasingly burdensome upon the parish, and measures were taken to bridge the fiscal gaps. Upon Fr. Ben's arrival, school enrollment, morale, and vision were waning. . . but "turning the tide" became the much-needed motivation. Crusading for Catholic education would become a primary objective and maxim resonating throughout his tenure at Christ the King. To date, three-and four-year-old pre-K programs have commenced, reinstated high school grade levels and a high school wing have been added to the campus, as well as a new library, playground, and science laboratory. A school foundation oversees endowments and charitable contributions. Christ the King Cathedral School will graduate fifteen seniors in May 2011, highlighted by a second consecutive senior class trip to Rome, Italy. The school's successful vantage points continue to build as students compete in scholastics, athletics, and extracurricular activities, garnering the Trojans citywide acclaim.

As part of the vision for continued growth in Catholic education, Fr. Ben advocated the need for an early childhood development program to retain families with infant children through high school adolescents. As vision took hold that required campus expansion, enthusiasm grew for a capital campaign that would include not only an early childhood education facility, but also a second gymnasium/events center, classrooms for adult education and meetings, and fellowship rooms for youth and college age ministries. This period of cathedral history, initiated with "Vision 20/20" objectives in 2003, is currently well underway. The beautiful multi-purpose facility is in use, with a second capital campaign being formalized.

As noted earlier in the memoirs, Fr. Ben began Christ Renews His Parish weekend retreats just sixteen months after arrival at Christ the King Cathedral. These alternating retreats for women, men and couples continued for three-and-one-half years, cultivating broad-based lay leadership and cross-generational spiritual growth. This spiritual rejuvenation prompted Perpetual Adoration, now in its ninth year cycle, as well as two additional commissions on the parish council, Spiritual Life and Youth Ministry. Expanding parish life and vision likewise precipitated three additional full-time staff positions, Youth Director, Development Director, and DRE/Family Outreach Director.

Much has been said of Fr. Ben's affirmation of women in ministerial positions. Of equal note at Christ the King Cathedral is the establishment of Spirituality for Men and This Man is You, as well as anticipation of four current diaconate candidates and spouses (to be ordained fall 2012) to join two existing deacons and wives already impacting multiple dimensions of community life. The cathedral parish has hosted seven associate priests during Fr. Ben's tenure, all contributing unique talents and much-needed respite for the pastor.

In the midst of these noteworthy years, on January 16, 2004, His Holiness John Paul II bestowed the title Prelate of Honor upon the pilgrim priest. From the French *monseigneur*, meaning "My Lord," the title is usually conferred on outstanding members of the local clergy, and is conferred on the recipient for his lifetime: our beloved Reverend Monsignor Bernardus Kasteel.

As we close these chapters of Msgr. Ben's life, with yet more to unfold, it reads like a "pilgrim's progress." Three continents, nine languages, five cultures, numerous parish families, diocesan and even Vatican recognition --- for what more could a priest ask? In the case of one formed in the spirit of Nazareth. . . simple joys, service as needed, tamales on Christmas Eve.

Prelate of Honor bestowed by Pope John Paul II
Celebration for Reverend Monsignor Ben Kasteel
2004

Christ the King Cathedral - Super Auction
Singing *"New York, New York"* to raise
money with Msgr. Gene Driscoll

Msgr. Ben with
graduate from
kindergarten
Christ the King
Cathedral School
May 2007

A: We have talked about your pilgrimage through many different historical stages and the effects upon your priestly vocation. Yet one of the most consequential eras through which you have pastored has been the public disgrace of sexual misconduct among the priesthood. I feel it is important to discuss your views on, and the ramifications of, this period of Church history.

B: I am completely open to discussion, but would like to start not at the point of priest scandal, but at the beginning of the story in the nineteen sixties with the sexual revolution. So let's go back to the sexual revolution in America, a reaction really all over the world, against long-standing assumptions that certain subjects were not to be discussed in public. In the sixties, topics once private were raised and discussed in open air, behaviors acted out with little censorship. On the national level, sexual promiscuity portrayed in movies and on TV led to an erosion of the sanctity of marriage and family as taught by the Church, dealing long-term consequences to the Church and state as well. Church matters such as birth control, should priests get married, the goal of marriage just for children, separation of sexes in Catholic education, homosexuality within the priesthood, etc., were also deeply influenced by this new sexual leniency.

I was actually serving on a council of Marist priests

in Washington, D.C., in the 1980's when the issue of homosexual tendencies within the priesthood came to the forefront at our seminary in Lafayette, Louisiana. The Marists immediately took action in the sense of protecting the people and trying to get the priests treatment and so on. In these early stages we could see the need to have legal people involved, and began to focus upon prevention as a primary objective.

A: Would you say there was a naivete within the magisterium before national publicity took center stage?

B: I can only speak as a priest at that time, and we rarely had thought about misconduct among our fellow priests. It was a difficult adjustment of becoming more cautious, say during my assignment at the Diocese of Wheeling, trying to watch clergy and their behavior, particularly in relationship with children in the school, children in high school, and so it became a kind of scrutiny, trying to be more aware of situations.

When the United States Conference of Catholic Bishops came together in Dallas in June 2002, and approved the Charter for Protection of Children and Young People, there was no doubt that sexual misconduct had to be addressed openly and decisively. It was already clear that, because the Catholic Church is one universal entity, the pain suffered by one diocese was really being suffered by all. Not only emotionally and spiritually, but financially. It became very much a money issue as lawyers became more and more involved, knowing that in the Catholic Church everything is connected so one can easily sue from one diocese to another. It became a kind of playing field. . . here is a place where you really can get money.

I know that in the beginning, the clergy and bishops were blamed for thinking the problem could be dealt with in much the same way as alcoholism. Someone with this illness was treated, then came back with skills for changed behavior and things would be alright. Later it became clear that you cannot compare alcoholic illness and treatment with sexual problems and consequences.

Before Vatican II, the clergy were very much on the pedestal, very much separated from the people. Then came the sexual revolution and the changes of Vatican II. The laity became much more involved in parish work, more friendships, more interaction between priests and laity, men and women. We moved from the extreme of social isolation to being encouraged to have friendships and even love relationships. . . too much permission to let down our social barriers without being prepared for our own, and others', vulnerability in a closer relational context.

A: During your tenure at Christ the King Cathedral, the national disclosure reached its full intensity. How did the Diocese of Lubbock respond, and were you involved?

B: In the Diocese of Lubbock a special board was convened to review allegations of any type of sexual misconduct. This was very painful, to deal with our own priests, our own deacons, in review of any type of construed misconduct on a very wide scope. I would say that in every family there are problems to be dealt with, there is no perfect place in the world, and it's the same within the priesthood. All sinfulness does not disappear, as priest you don't become a perfect person.

The Diocese of Lubbock focused upon creating and assuring safe environments, within our parish life and especially for the children. All teachers and all personnel within Catholic schools are now trained for safe environment, and all children of the schools receive special instruction regarding self-protection. An ongoing diocesan review board handles all inquiries with reference to sexual misconduct.

I think the financial costs have been huge, but the much more serious result has been the enormous hurt done to families and to children. It is surely a dark page in the history of the Catholic Church, but I can see slowly things have settled down, good reforms have come as a result.

A: Please give some examples of "good reforms" that have come following the investigations, reports and responses.

B: The emphasis on safe environments as mentioned above, not just to lock up places, but how you should respect each other. Training that is required to work in any capacity, even as a volunteer, with our children and youth. Candidates for the priesthood are being more thoroughly evaluated and more thoroughly educated, which includes sexual and human development. There is renewed commitment to chastity within all levels of Church life, emphasizing the need to discipline and control oneself as opposed to the sexual permissiveness of our culture. The accountability that has ensued to recognize and address sexual problems with knowledgeable counselors and lifelong treatment. Ensuring that human development of the whole person, not just intellectual and spiritual development, has to take place and applies within seminaries. And I believe the priesthood has gone through a resurrection of deeper spirituality.

A: How would you describe what the Church, the institution, has been through?

B: I think that the Church went through a real suffering, and there is still a lot of suffering because you have many priests who made a mistake who are extremely sorry for it, who are out of ministry now. Among the laity are adults and children who are deeply wounded by the violation and shame of abuse. When Pope Benedict XVI came to America, he apologized to every audience within his itinerary for the hurt that was created. We can never apologize enough. It's like with everything, one person can do more harm that one hundred people can do good. Healing is a slow process, but God wants that our painful wounds become holy wounds.

And out of these holy wounds, I think God wants us to live into the future. We have to face what's done wrong in the past, and have to start to live for the future and make the best of the years to come. That is what God wants us to do. And as a priest I say that to every person. When I counsel someone who has been through a tragedy, I say you have experienced what it did to you personally, you know what kind of guilt and anger it creates. I think now you can be the best person talking to others living in the midst of pain and tragedy. Your wounds may be healing for someone else. God's will is not in the tragic actions that take place, but His will is in how we deal with it. Turn darkness into light.

THE PARABLE OF THE TEN
VIRGINS. "Then the kingdom of
heaven will be like ten virgins who took
their lamps and went out to meet the
bridegroom. Five of them were foolish
and five were wise. The foolish ones,
when taking their lamps, brought no
oil with them, but the wise brought
flasks of oil with their lamps. Since the
bridegroom was long delayed, they all
became drowsy and feel asleep.

At midnight, there was a cry, 'Behold,
the bridegroom! Come out to meet him!'
Then all those virgins got up and trimmed
their lamps. The foolish ones said to
the wise, 'Give us some of your oil, for
our lamps are going out.' But the wise
ones replied, 'No, for there may not be
enough for us and you. Go instead to the
merchants and buy some for yourselves.'

While they went off to buy it, the
bridegroom came and those who were
ready went into the wedding feast
with him. Then the door was locked.
Afterwards the other virgins came and
said, 'Lord, Lord, open the door for us!'
But he said in reply, 'Amen, I say to
you, I do not know you.' Therefore, stay
awake, for you know neither the day nor
the hour."

Matthew 25:1-13

The parable of the ten virgins recalls a beloved
Jewish tradition, the procession and continuous feasting
that encompassed up to an entire week following
the marriage ceremony. This custom allowed for
bridesmaids, or "virgins," to keep watch for the coming
of the bridegroom, who often came unexpectedly in
the middle of night. Upon his coming, their lamps
would light the way, insuring the bridegroom's entrance
through the gate where the bride and guests would be
waiting. Shortly after the bridegroom entered, the gate
would be closed, allowing no discretionary late entry
until the week-long festivities concluded. (9)

This was a time of great merriment to which all
would aspire, setting the stage for a parable about the
virtue of being prepared. Those listening to Jesus' story
knew well the consequences of missing the crucial and
limited time of admittance through the gate.

Out of a group of ten bridesmaids in this parable,
five were prepared and five were not. Five participated
in the festivities; five were excluded after attempting (in
haste) to get their lamps in working condition. Had the
unprepared only been zealous about the need to carry
oil, the foresight to take responsibility for their personal

lamps to illumine the way, theirs would have been the week of feasting.

In the previous pages of Msgr. Ben's history at Christ the King, one sees both the luminosity surrounding parish life, and the darkness occurring nationwide as abuse was disclosed. Potential for light and darkness. . . coexisting. . . right up until the opening of the gate. This parable alerts the faithful: be prepared. You each carry a lamp, but you must also be carrying the oil!

Story has been the perennial means by which people of faith pass along truth. We see the story or parable's truth for ourselves in each subsequent generation. At Christ the King, during our current history, Msgr. Ben has steadfastly prepared the lamp that leads us through the gate. He has done this daily by carrying his own supply of oil. He has done this by knowing that darkness has the potential to thwart what God has planned for us. He has been vigilant in his own preparation, seeing in this parable that one cannot borrow oil from one's neighbor! We do well to see in his watchfulness that nothing should be taken for granted. Crucial moments of light and darkness come unexpectedly, sometimes in public arenas, sometimes behind closed doors.

And we, the all-inclusive faithful of the Roman Catholic Church, should not be averse to identifying ourselves with those virgins found unprepared.

Why? Because living with a repentant heart is the perpetual dimension of our Catholic faith. This is how we prepare the way of the Lord. This is the perspective from which we begin each Mass. This is our posture as we approach the Eucharistic table, "Lord, I am not worthy that you should enter under my roof, but only say the word and my soul shall be healed." (10) The sacred season of Lent writes its penitent word on our remorseful souls, and collectively we take upon ourselves as community the truth of David's psalm:

> *For I know my offense; my sin is always before me. Against you alone have I sinned; I have done such evil in your sight. . . (11)*

As Msgr. Ben has said, "We (the entire Church) can never apologize enough." *Perdóname. . . Perdóname . . . forgive me.* Ours is the lesson of unpreparedness, a darkness with devastating consequences. With humble and contrite hearts as Church, we are embraced by Paschal Mystery . . . we die, we rise, receiving the Spirit for one who was without oil. We turn darkness into light.

Heather Ruiz
Middle School Art Teacher

media: liquid pen

"I wanted to convey Monsignor Ben's journey; his past, present, and walking into his future."

CHAPTER TEN
Compass Chart

At the close of this memoirs project, I encouraged Msgr. Ben's comments toward the future. As he mused over advice for future seminarians (and their families!), the Catholic Church's presence within an ever more integrated world, and his vision for the Cathedral parish, I found his enthusiasm contagious. Even more surprising, I find myself as a Catholic laywoman competent and compelled to do something regarding all of the above.

Why would a laywoman, Protestant convert imagine herself as an crusader for the Catholic Church of the future? I am an unlikely prospect and yet cannot walk away from the ties that bind me to this vehicle of faith. I am guarded toward many of the dogmas and hierarchic structure that "drive the bus" I am riding. My frustrations rise seeing the palpable apathy at the bus stops along the way. . . so few boarding to go the distance. And then the feeling that we are going in circles, in small circumferences that refuse to stretch out into uncharted domain. I could despair over my tiny voice from the back of the bus influencing the driver, much less to turn down a path toward revision of some long-standing practices. Why do I stay on a route that seems to be predictably mapped out, by an all-male navigational system?

I stay because historically it is not a predictable map at all. In my own lifetime, the premier example is the Second Vatican Council. The truth is that no one can say about the Catholic Church, "That's the way it has always been." Variety has been more the rule than uniformity. There have been great variations as to the role of the pope, the liturgy of the Mass, clerical lifestyles and popular devotions. There have been many schools of theological thought and numerous variations in the sacraments (12). This much evidence convinces me that this vehicle of faith, my Church, does consistently make adjustments in its "mapquest" . . . and if I exit, I might miss an eye-opening, future-impacting vista around the next corner!

And I stay on board because of the pride I feel being connected to Catholic heritage. My life is so enriched under the guidance of mystics and saints, within the context of monastic prayer, among the faithful (past, present and future) in communion at the Eucharistic table, around the rural mission churches that dot the Texas countryside. . . an encompassing embrace by a Church all too human, yet full of light. As priests and religious model for me an obedience within institutional religion, they also exemplify for me the journey toward spiritual transformation I cannot find elsewhere. No other Christian denomination demands that one hold the tension as does the Catholic Church; under its umbrella, far-right to far-left and a huge array of cultural and ethnic diversity belong. "In this modern day and age, when the life and dignity of the human person is being threatened at almost every turn, the Catholic Church remains the world's premier institutional defender of human rights." (13) We share a creed that defines us and a sacramental life that nourishes us (with priests making that possible!).

If there is any place for this errant woman's voice and life on this bus, and there is, then I will ride alongside my community and be reminded what it means to hold the tension of authentic gospel imperatives. Most certainly this means, with the help of brothers and sisters, setting the course toward simplicity of lifestyle, peacemaking, eco-consciousness, non-violence, serving the "least of these among us," and a discipline of prayer that undergirds each day --- just to mention a few. And then the commission to teach, to suffer the issues (e.g., immigration reform, abortion), to fast and practice almsgiving. . . feel the gospel tension beckon us down a road less traveled? This is, in part, the discernment process for all men and women, particularly those considering a vocational call. Are we, the collective Church of the future, doing all we can to make this counter-cultural road a destination for more and more?

In thanksgiving for all the years in the priesthood —
Msgr. Ben with beloved colleagues

A: We have reached the present moment in our reflection of your pilgrim journey. Looking back, there have been circumstances you never anticipated.

B: But that is often the best part, or where God's hand becomes so visible. You can make all kind of plans, set goals, etc., but you have to be available when things happen that were not foreseen. When George W. Bush became President, he never imagined the country coming under the attacks of 9/11. Events that happen in the world, or even in a parish, start to kind of lead your life, and you follow a path of obedience to that.

A: So then the process of discernment must be guided by the moment?

B: Yes. For your surrender to the unexpected.

A: How would you advise someone considering a vocational call to the priesthood to understand this concept?

B: This is the way God calls, it is the way I see God calls . . . in the smallest and biggest of ways. For example, on a Sunday afternoon you just finish Mass, just had something to eat and then a phone call, emergency call at a hospital. You would love to sit down. Human nature, right? But then you think, "No, it's a soul. I go. I go."

That kind of availability, of obedience, comes out of the ministry. Other times you just sit down, put your feet up and the phone rings, somebody wants to talk, needs to talk. So the priestly ministry is much the same as the life of a mother. There are many inconvenient moments.

A: And you find yourself, as did St. Paul, saying the words, "In my weakness, You are strong." Is this kind of vulnerability taught or learned?

B: In truth I see my whole life as many teachable moments, where I had to learn to open myself in order to accept the need of the circumstances. Say in the islands, you arrive from seminary thinking you already know what everything is, but the longer you are there you admit, "No, I don't know." You would be a very narrow person not to allow the people to tell you about the customs. . . you need them to explain to you, and the longer you wait to ask and listen, the more time is wasted in being unable to communicate, adapt, hopefully incorporate a priestly presence in their midst.

It happened the same when I came to United States to learn the American customs. You just have to be open, try to understand and apply yourself to it. And the same when I arrived in Plainview, I had to learn a whole style, way of life, how Hispanics come together, what is important to them, learn their celebrations, learn their lifestyle. Even coming here to Christ the King, from parish to parish, you learn something different through a competent staff and often highly educated lay people, and a community with much greater resources than any place I previously served.

And I would say any meeting that I attend. . . meetings, meetings, meetings!. . . in every meeting I learn something. If you're a little bit open to learn things you didn't know before, you see so many teachable moments. I think you have to be open to it. That is maybe one of the privileges of a priest, to appreciate the lessons in each context.

A: The general perception is that the laity is learning from you. They would see themselves as the students, you as the teacher.

B: The opposite is just as true. Yes, the priest teaches things he has studied about scripture, theology, sacraments, Church history, spirituality, etc. But just knowing these things does not necessarily prepare you to deal with real life, and in this respect, the laity know as much, maybe more, than priests. I know that maybe some priests are threatened by this. I also think some younger priests are threatened by entering a parish where the laity is well informed, or has a lot of talent and specialized professions.

But this will always be the case. Seminary cannot possibly teach all there is to know about experiencing God, oneself and Church, working with people, and running a business. When I attended seminary we were not prepared for business administration, everything was much more simple lifestyle. Now a parish is a big business. A priest today does not have to be a financial manager, but he has to know the pastoral aspects of finances. Always in the mind of the priest are issues of poverty and charity, so when evaluating tight budgets there is still a priority to help the poor and needy. At Christ the King, I must also take the financial needs of the school into consideration, and this calls for a special responsibility in pastoral leadership.

A: There are so many considerations for young men discerning a vocational call to the priesthood. What would you point to as a stumbling block in the process?

B: The first stumbling block is within one's own family. I mean not many people, very few families, are really in favor of their son becoming priest today. Most families have two or three children, and they say they would like to have grandchildren for themselves, so that is one of the issues. Also parents can see so many opportunities in today's world, living the American dream, promising success and financial rewards for their children. Too many choices. . . travel, education, family life, financial gain, master of destiny. . . a parent sees all of these as positives, and the life of a priest full of sacrifice, obedience, lack of personal fulfillment, isolation from relationships. Funny that I actually gained many of the positive things in my choice to become priest. Education, travel, family life (because I was in religious community) and a great deal of personal fulfillment were all in my life as priest. I feel extremely blessed to have been spared many disillusions the world would have us believe are paths to happiness. Too much stuff, too much stimulation. Parents can model the benefits of simplicity by example, choosing silence at times, less-is-more as a way of life. Self-surrender seen and taught as a positive enhances the common good of people and of the environment.

A: Moving from the past, through the present, I would like to close in pointing toward the future. What do you think is the biggest issue the Church faces on the world level?

B: I think what our present Pope is working on. . . Benedict XVI and the dialogue between the Catholic Church and Islam. We have many things in common with Muslims, and because their religion has such a worldwide presence, it is extremely important for dialogue to create a greater unity between us. I also expect Pope Benedict XVI to make major strides toward closer relationship with the Eastern Orthodox church. And because our world is so connected by technology, the Catholic "universal" presence in Africa, South America and China is entering the dialogue as never before. It is also of utmost concern how Europe will maintain its Catholic identity. Right now it is hard to see how secularism will play out, if the tide will turn and people will come home to faith. If I look in history there is always a moment when God brings forward a great saint, who really starts to move a country. . . like St. Francis and the Little Brothers in Italy, who really bring people back to church. Just a thought.

And, of course, I think the future of the Eucharist, as we know it, is at stake. I come from Holland, and I see that the shortness of priests has caused the collapse of receiving regular Eucharist in many parishes. When in Samoa I took care of seven to nineteen parishes, my pastor at home (Holland) takes care of twelve parishes. This means the communion service is more the people's experience than Mass.

A: And on the local level, what would you anticipate as future vision for Christ the King Cathedral?

B: First, to uphold its role as cathedral. Say, by example, the diocese has a responsibility to lead in all kind of ministries, to help and so on. The cathedral is the place where the bishop could say is an example for all the parishes, and it should take a greater responsibility in the formation of the laity. Adult education should be a top priority. . . connecting scripture with the teachings of the Church, theology and morality, Christian spirituality and Catholic apologetics. . . making these available and promoted within parish life. The programs should be so good that it attracts people to come, programs created because people really want and see it as needed. We have many examples already at Christ the King, of successful programs that were born from laity leadership.

On the agenda for the next diaconate class (ordained in 2012) is the development of lay ministry. Perhaps using deanery organization, deacons can help lay people be trained, get a stronger foundation and background in their chosen ministries. Catechists and youth ministers, those who reach out to sick and homebound, people that love to work in certain areas --- that they get the opportunity, can work with the priests, and/or volunteer on the diocesan level. In this way build confidence, that laypeople can lead and minister to others, empowered and commissioned by the Church.

And in the old days, the cathedral was a center of fine art and music. Pope Benedict XVI is promoting a return to art in Catholic churches, in modern times overlooked because of emphasis on quick and efficient methods of building facilities. Art and music can be a most dynamic symbol of faith, moving us to contemplation and prayer, and a beautiful way for Christ the King Cathedral to interact with the Lubbock community at large.

A: From your beginning in missionary work to Monsignor at the cathedral parish, is there a sense of what is important for you to accomplish in the time you have left as an active priest? Is it pastoral? Is it growth? Is it the school? Is it team building? Is it empowering those that are coming behind you?

B: It is to come. Really excellent programs that will create a new vibration. It will not have much to do with me, and I am really not concerned about what I accomplish. I am more interested in how this parish can become fully alive. Like the Bible says, "a Holy Nation, a Holy People". . . . sanctification of the people. We are shifting from suburban to city parish, we have a mixture of different ages, cultures, economics. I would like to see how we can strengthen the children, from the earliest moment bring Catholic spirituality into their lives. And to do all we can to strengthen family life in this parish, strengthen families. That is what I would say I am most concerned about.

As priests approach retirement, usually around age seventy-five if in good health, we have our dreams. The dreams are not always to do more, but how can what we do become deeper. . . more authentic. I hope this dream will stay the center of my ministry, especially in regards to the school. I have this kind of formal prayer that I pray every day, that Divine Mercy come upon our school, upon the whole parish, families, single parents and married parents. That the Lord truly brings this, leads the people to happiness of life and to family closeness. I believe Christ rejoices when He sees the family get together, celebrate together.

I am not interested in just finishing my time at Christ the King maintaining what is in place. I must be about the work of spiritual development, and no better place than at the school with their dedication to form the best of people. The same with the youth organization, in whatever way I can help build the spiritual foundation that will last the rest of these young people's lives. From beginning to end, this has been my call. . . prayer and mission, the mixture of both, that leads all of us to holiness.

PARABLES OF THE KINGDOM:
"The kingdom of heaven is like a treasure
buried in a field, which a person finds
and hides again, and out of joy goes
and sells all that he has and buys that
field. Again, the kingdom of heaven is
like a merchant searching for fine pearls.
When he finds a pearl of great price, he
goes and sells all that he has and buys
it. Again, the kingdom of heaven is like
a net thrown into the sea, which collects
fish of every kind. When it is full they
haul it ashore and sit down to put what
is good into buckets. What is bad they
throw away."

Matthew 13:44-48

In this parable concerning the kingdom of heaven
we find common truth in all three examples:
1) what is being searched for is not visible to the naked
eye; and, 2) what is found is of immense value, worth a
great price to attain.

The treasure, the pearl, and the bounty of fish all
come to the seeker as a result of intentional seeking and
intentional effort. . . these gems are not stumbled upon.

There is no reference as to how long the search has been going on, but we can see that joy and redefinition of what is valuable come as a result of the discovery.

I am reminded of one particular quest on the Samoan Islands, as told by Msgr. Ben, in his earliest years of the priesthood. The object of his desire was the piece of paper upon which his homily had been written (in Samoan-speak). His intent was sincere and his search was arduous, but to no avail. The paper was, indeed, at the main station, he and his waiting congregation across the mountains. What he did discover was his capacity to preach without notes. . . a "pearl" for the upcoming forty-seven years, becoming "treasure" for his parishioners.

Though we sometimes "collect fish" in our cast nets, by design we are a faith family of perennial seekers. . . knowing there is more, longing for what is beyond our grasp, searching for what will satisfy our emptiness. The Hebrew and Christian scriptures are full of seekers, illustrated by: Moses for land flowing with milk and honey; David for God's own heart; the shepherds, wise men, and King Herod for the newborn baby; Nicodemus for eternal life. Some of these found and retained what they were looking for, some did not. Scores of searchers are left to lament, as found in Bono's lyrics of the famous U2 song, "I Still Haven't Found What I'm Looking For."

What is a Catholic Christian entering a new century to do? A vast number will determine they have already obtained all there is of value in organized religion and look elsewhere, especially if they have not glimpsed a spark or felt a vibration during their once-a-week attendance. But many will be stirred to an intentional exploration. . . and I would point to our own backyard in which to commence digging.

I would suggest we excavate the past. . . not to bring back to life some historical way of being, but to inform ourselves into the future. We would find a Church that is historically full of paradox and accustomed to change, and in this gain confidence for the future. We have not been given all the answers, as we see that no period of history has had all the answers. We are not lost, nor are we finished. . . we are in process, a pilgrim people of movement, journey and change. With an in-depth and honest study of Church history, we can acknowledge that the Church of Constantine was different from the Church of Peter and Paul, the Church of Vatican I different from the Church of Trent, and the list goes on and on. Yes, the Church of Vatican II is different from the post-Reformation Church, and as in all the other centuries of change, the transition is not made without considerable pain and hardship. (14)

Fear not, ye faithful! This is our history from which

we draw inspiration and in which we plumb our future identity. If we determine the priesthood must undergo change in order to preserve the full expression of Eucharist at every Mass. . . fear not! The structure of the clergy has not always been as we know it now (in earlier forms included married men, and in earlier forms did not dress different than laity). For that matter, the bread of Eucharist did not always take the form of the small, round white host as we know it, first introduced in the eighth century.

As stated by William J. Bausch in *Pilgrim Church:*

> To be Catholic is to have a large and long 'context' in which to assess the modern world. To be Catholic is to evaluate the present in the light of the past, to be sensitive to what moved the people then -- what were their inspirations, motivations and their spirit -- that we might recapture such for ourselves. (15)

In doing so we find not so much a historical institution as we find a historical people who molded and shaped, persistently, the enduring institution.

None within its ranks have been more influential than those historical people we call "priest." To them we owe our firsthand, validating experiences of faith, through the sacraments over which they preside that initiate, heal, nourish, absolve, confirm, relinquish and unite us in the love of Christ. Each has been a sojourner, not fully understanding where the journey will lead, but knowing The Voice that calls. . . and following the priestly archetype of Samuel, has responded, "Here I am, Lord. Send me." The deep kinship we cherish around the Eucharist table has come through the Bread and the Cup at their hands for twenty centuries. How can we express gratitude more effectively than taking upon ourselves the serious task of building community and vocations as their legacy?

Thus we affirm the pilgrimage that remains for all. Our collective objective is to "dig. . . find. . . cast our nets" for this authentic historical process to both *preserve* and *create*. Our collective goal is to equip ourselves with an in-depth understanding of unedited Church history (using the "vibrant" programming wished for by Msgr. Ben), being confident there is a past that lives on through each of us.

Afterword

Dear Ben,

As we celebrate your retirement, I would just like to share with you some thoughts and appreciation I have for the Lord bringing you into the pilgrimage of my life.

July 1971, we met at the Cleveland airport as you arrived to begin another segment of your priestly ministry. I remember that the oils of my own priesthood were still penetrating my being. You impressed me with the energetic zeal you showed me for our priestly ministry as we embarked on a beautiful friendship of discipleship together.

You have been a good mentor and an example for all priests. The secret of your generosity is found, without a doubt, in your love for God, Mary, and the people entrusted to your care.

The priestly service you have shared for the forty-seven years of your ministry has been a true witness for Christ and His church. I know it has reflected on the many souls you have enriched with His grace. Your availability to serve has been a blessing to the Society of Mary and the Diocese of Lubbock.

Thank you for your contributions in teaching us God's plan and salvation.

As you reach another phase of your priestly life, I wish you the best. I pray you can enjoy this segment to continue to read and relax. We know we will be looking forward to some fun times together.

Well done, good and faithful friend --- let us continue the journey. I guess we better invest in a GPS to show us our travels.

God Bless you and Keep You in His Care!
Your friend,

Gene (Msgr. Gene Driscoll)

A few days vacation in Palo Duro Canyon State Park
in the Texas panhandle near Amarillo

My name is Maria Rodriguez. I worked with Msgr. Ben Kasteel as secretary at Our Lady of Guadalupe church in Plainview, Texas, from 1990-1998. I learned how to speak and write English while working with him. I grew in my faith. Msgr. Ben helped me to be a better person, and to believe in myself. That is one of his many talents, he never gives up on people. He has faith in everybody. There is not a bad person for him in this world. I looked forward to going to work every morning. There were no bad days at work with Msgr. Ben. He always had a word of encouragement, or just by looking at him in church praying every morning, that would make my day.

Everybody loved Msgr. Ben in Our Lady of Guadalupe. They were very thankful for everything he did in the community. The church was a small mission in the barrio of Plainview with just a few families involved whenever Msgr. Ben came to Plainview. He helped to buy the old City National Bank building downtown and made it into a church. In the 10 years that I worked there we had close to 800 families registered in the parish, thanks to Msgr. Ben, because he believed anything could be possible if we had enough faith. Everybody loves him and he is well remembered in Our Lady of Guadalupe in Plainview.

There are many personal accounts and stories in my life. He is like a real father to me. I remember the day he took me to get my driver's license. The day I got married, he prepared a meal for my husband and me at his house. Whenever I had each of my children he was so happy, as though they were his own grandchildren. He always had a big sign of WELCOME! in the office when we came back to work. My children grew up in the office. Until now there is not a birthday or Christmas that he will forget to send a card to us. He is part of our family. We love him.

Another special event that I remember and helps me in my faith, is a time when we didn't have enough money to give the church payment. That morning I asked him what we were going to do and he said, "I don't know but the day is not over yet." I saw him going to church with a book in his hand to pray. Later on that day a person came to bring a donation of $5,000. To me that was a miracle, to him that was just faith in God. That is how strong his faith is. The best words of encouragement that have been very helpful in my life are, "You got to live **DAY BY DAY**." I love Msgr. Ben and I pray that God bless him in his ministry.

Maria Rodriguez (holding her son),
Secretary to Fr. Ben in Plainview
Lupe Villarreal, her younger sister (on right) now serves as
Youth Director at Christ the King Cathedral

Coming from an ecumenical background, I entered Catholicism with preconceived notions about the priesthood. Mostly I imagined "men of the cloth" to be guardians of the faith. . . which was somewhat intimidating for one who, as an adult, was just beginning to learn about sacraments, holy days of obligation, communion of saints, etc. I felt like a adolescent who did not want to be called on by the teacher, yet desperately wanted to contribute something of value to the community table.

So it was this longing that drove me to schedule a meeting with Fr. Ben about one year after his arrival at Christ the King. I was perplexed and seeking wisdom regarding my place in parish life; I didn't know where to cast my nets. This was the encounter that enlarged my perception of the priesthood. I returned home verbalizing to my family, "Now I know why we call them *Fathers*."

In the years since this discovery, I have repeatedly encountered clerical wisdom, wit, compassion, conviviality, sensitivity, discernment, affirmation and courage. . . all within my one-diocese-circumference of the priesthood. And since that initial meeting, I have been challenged multiple times by this spiritual Father under my parish roof to step up to the plate, step out on a limb, and step into the depths of Christian mystery.

The tables turned nearly three years ago, when it was I who presented the challenge of a memoirs project to my esteemed pastor. His immediate response was disinterest at anything that focused upon him. "I never intend for there to be a book about me.". . yet the Spirit persuaded him that it would really be a book *about the priesthood*. Our mutual objective has been attained when the resulting text illumines a path of ministry, particularly for readers and their families discerning ordination or consecrated lives within our Church.

At the close of this fruitful collaboration, I offer a quote in tribute to Msgr. Ben's odyssey of faith:

> Pilgrims are persons in motion --- passing through territories not their own --- seeing something we might call completion, or perhaps the word clarity will do as well, a goal to which only the spirit's compass points the way. (16)

May God continue to bless the road that rises up to meet his vocational call!

Ann Krier

Ann Krier, scribe of these recollections

Ann Krier with Msgr. Ben
in one of many taped interviews

Acknowledgments

For two millennia, Mother Church has raised up sons skilled in the priestly tasks of our sacramental life. Because of the priesthood, Kingdom is closer, chasms are reconciled, participation is affirmed, hope is proclaimed. These recollections gratefully acknowledge the prayers and actions of all the priests with us and for us throughout our history, affirming the legacy to be carried forward.

So it is to Msgr. Ben, the quiet man who never waivered, I give my deepest appreciation. . . on behalf of all who have followed his lead, sat in his presence, sought his counsel, and taken his dare to be all we are created to be.

Throughout the emergence period of three years, God has provided significant others to birth this memoirs project. My heartfelt indebtedness:

To Bishop Placido Rodriguez and Msgr. Gene Driscoll. . . the colleagues (amigos!) with whom Msgr. Ben came to call "home" the Diocese of Lubbock.

To Elizabeth Matthews and Susan Collier. . . the "alpha" and "omega" technicians who brought the recorded spoken words from beginning to end in the publication being held.

To Laney Bridwell, Amy Anderson, Pat Leach, Joan Hegdal, Marty Martin. . . the faithful proofreaders, whose feedback and affirmation propelled the project ever forward.

To Heather Ruiz and her middle school advanced art students. . . the talented visionaries who created cover designs and chapter introductions out of their admiration for Monsignor Ben.

To the sojourners traveling with me to the monastery when Monsignor called. . . the sweet inspiration we shared has remained a guiding light.

To my husband, Steve, and staunchest supporter. . . whose abundant confidence pilots this woman toward expansive horizons.

And most assuredly to SarahLee Morris. . . whose expertise of written word combined with bona fide joy of spiritual expression birthed this dream into reality.

To my earthly father, now deceased, whose life story was a precursor.

And to our Father/Mother God, who plants seeds and grows all things according to sacred time and place. May the blessings of vocations be cultivated through all these hands and according to Your purpose.

Notes

1. William J. Bausch, Pilgrim Church:
   A Popular History of Catholic Christianity
   (Mystic: Twenty-Third Publications, 1981),
   p. 535.

2. Ibid., pp. 536-537.

3. William Barclay, *The Parables of Jesus*
   (Louisville: Westminster John Knox Press, 1999),
   p. 127.

4. Marianne Williamson, *A Return to Love:
   Reflections on the Principles of A Course in
   Miracles* (Harper Collins, 1992), pp. 190-191.

5. See Matthew 6:5-6, 11-12; Mark 8:15; Luke 12:1;
   I Corinthians 5:6-8; Galatians 5:9.

6. Thomas Merton, *New Seeds of Contemplation*
   (New York: New Directions Paperbooks, 1972),
   p. 173.

7. Ibid., pp. 173-174.

8. See Wisdom 9; Proverbs 8:22-31; Sirach 24:1-9.

9. William Barclay, pp. 133-135.

10. See *Ecce Agnus Dei*: *Excerpts from the English
    translation of* The Roman Missal *Copyright 2010
    United States Conference of Catholic Bishops,
    Washington, D.C.*

11. See Psalm 51:5-6a.

12. William J. Bausch, pp. 540-541.

13. Matthew Kelly, *Rediscover Catholicism* (Beacon Publishing, 2010), pp. 21-22.

14. William J. Bausch, pp. 542-543.

15. Ibid., p. 544.

16. Richard R. Niebuhr, *Pioneers and Pilgrims* In: <u>Parabola,</u> (IX:3; Fall, 1984), p. 7.

Middle School Advanced Art Class
Christ the King Cathedral School
Spring 2011

Standing, left to right: Sarah Settle, Catherine Limboy,
Sophia Velasquez, Nikki Diaz, Joseph Marzak,
Charles Lascano, Elena Luera, Abbigail Hines,
Sidney Herrera, Brenna Lumongsud

Back Cover Design of Samoan Islands by:
Sarah Settle, 6th Grade
media: watercolor; India ink
(see page 63)